"Built on important and well-recogni... ...m-
ples, *Smart Compassion* provides pat... ...be
with and walk with people. The read... ...nd
doing acts of charity to actions that ... ...into entering into the lives of
others in tangible ways. Read *Smart Compassion* and you will be ready to
answer its call to start waging shalom."
—**Steve Corbett, coauthor of *When Helping Hurts***

"If you want to make a difference in your community, you need to read this
book. Wesley Furlong is unique in that he is both a thought leader and a
practitioner. *Smart Compassion* is full of tools that will help you make a last-
ing impact."
—**Dave Runyon, coauthor of *The Art of Neighboring***

"'My people are destroyed for lack of knowledge' (Hosea 4:6). This verse
jumped out at me as I read *Smart Compassion*. I believe that Wesley Furlong
has given the church a treasure. It would do us well to dig deep, find the
treasure, and experience the authentic, transforming mission that God has for
us. This book is a timely word in season!"
—**Nelson Okanya, president of Eastern Mennonite Missions**

"Wesley Furlong's work and writing combine great storytelling with insights
and applications that will transform people and places. The concepts of healing presence, radical hospitality, and collective empowerment are a Christ-cen-
tered framework for life, church, and community transformation. A book
worth reading and, even more, worth living."
—**Brian D. Bennett, founder and pastor of Overflow Church**

"One size doesn't fit all when it comes to engaging needs of the people around
us. Wesley Furlong's work gives practical advice on how to customize your
response appropriately so that people are genuinely helped. This insight will
both free and fire you up! Your community will be glad you read this book!"
—**Reggie McNeal, author of *Missional Renaissance* and *Kingdom Come***

"The way to transformational renewal of your church, your organization, and
your own life as a follower of Jesus is clear and compelling in this exceptional
integration of biblical Christian faith and Christlike living. Wesley Furlong
shows us the way to act on the prayer that Jesus gave us: we want your kingdom to come here and now in this particular place and in me as it is in heaven.
If you really do want that prayer answered, read this book."
—**Richard Kriegbaum, president of Fresno Pacific University**

"*Smart Compassion* puts love for one's neighbor into shoe leather. Our life in faith is to be relational, first with our Lord but in turn with all whom we meet. This is a stimulating read."

—Myron Augsburger, president emeritus of Eastern Mennonite University

"For those who pay more than lip service to Jeremiah's call to seek the peace of the city, *Smart Compassion* comes at just the right moment. Its unique combination of on-the-ground realism and pragmatic tools equips us for new approaches to pursuing gospel-centered human flourishing in the context of actual communities. A great discussion starter for churches wishing for greater community engagement."

—Randy White, author of *Encounter God in the City*

"Don't read *Smart Compassion* if you want your church to remain safe and comfortable. Read it if you want to fully immerse yourself in God's plan for mercy, justice, and healing in your neighborhood."

—John M. Perkins, minister and bestselling author

"Love your neighbor: Jesus' simple command can take a lifetime to master. While there is no shortage of resources for Christians and churches about living out this command, I'm grateful for guidance that emphasizes relationships and incarnational ministry. That's what you get with Wesley Furlong's book: a smart approach to compassion that comes with a lot of heart."

—Richard Stearns, president of World Vision U.S. and author of *The Hole in Our Gospel*

"We are called to love the Lord our God with all of our heart, mind, soul, and strength—but too often, we forget to engage our minds. Wesley Furlong's new book is sobering and enlightening, a call to cultivate love and justice as we actively love our neighbors. Ultimately, *Smart Compassion* teaches us to love as Christ has loved us, bringing holistic transformation to our hearts and our minds."

—Peter Greer, president and CEO of HOPE International and coauthor of *Mission Drift*

"*Smart Compassion* captured my heart from the moment author Wesley Furlong asked us to consider this central question of how to spend your life well on behalf of others. Through careful examination of Scripture and practical steps, he invites and challenges us to consider what 'doing better' looks like. A great read!"

—Beth Guckenberger, cofounder of Back2Back Ministries and author of *Start with Amen*

smart com•pas•sion

\ˈsmärt kəm-ˈpa-shən\

▶ how to stop "doing outreach"
and start making change

wesley furlong

Herald Press

Harrisonburg, Virginia

Library of Congress Cataloging-in-Publication Data
Names: Furlong, J. Wesley, 1977- author.
Title: Smart compassion : how to stop doing outreach and start making change
 / Wesley Furlong.
Description: Harrisonburg : Herald Press, 2017. | Includes bibliographical
 references.
Identifiers: LCCN 2016043938| ISBN 9781513800394 (pbk. : alk. paper) |
ISBN
 9781513801346 (hardcover : alk. paper)
Subjects: LCSH: Communities--Religious aspects--Christianity. |
 Hospitality--Religious aspects--Christianity. | Compassion--Religious
 aspects--Christianity. | Church work. | Christian life.
Classification: LCC BV4517.5 .F87 2017 | DDC 261/.1--dc23 LC record avail-
able at https://lccn.loc.gov/2016043938

SMART COMPASSION
© 2017 by Herald Press, Harrisonburg, Virginia 22802. All rights reserved.
Library of Congress Control Number: 2016043938
International Standard Book Number: 978-1-5138-0039-4 (paper);
 978-1-5138-0134-6 (HC)
Printed in United States of America
Cover and layout by Reuben Graham

For orders or information, call 800-245-7894 or visit HeraldPress.com.

21 20 19 18 17   10 9 8 7 6 5 4 3 2 1

For Bonnie

How wonderful it is that nobody need wait a single moment before starting to improve the world.
—**Anne Frank**

Contents

Dragging the Piano into the Street

I once had a vision of a young family living in a city. Imagine this with me for a moment: Their neighborhood has just endured a lethal gun battle between rival gangs. But this young family neither cowers in fear nor calls a real estate agent nor moves immediately into fix-it mode. Instead, they pull their upright piano into the street. The mother sits down at the piano, and the family gathers around her. Together they begin to sing worship songs in the middle of the street. They sing full voice, with tears streaming down their faces. Neighbors look out their windows, and a few venture out onto the sidewalk. A couple of people eventually join in. And there, inside the police tape and on the doorstep of death, they hold a worship service. It is an act of supplication and defiance. Life will prevail! They worship and pray. They stand in death's valley and cry out to God for new life.

The next week, they begin to give themselves to what they sing for. Those gathered begin to meet together for prayer, fasting, and the pursuit of their community's flourishing. "God, may your kingdom come here as it is in heaven!" they pray. "Show us how to collaborate with what you're doing here to bring about new life." They meet with neighbors and community leaders, learn from others around the country, and begin to establish a collective healing presence in their neighborhood. They work with a spiritual sensitivity and a trustworthy strategy. In time, the neighborhood becomes a verdant place and a life-giving community.

This vision is a microcosm of smart compassion. Smart compassion is the full pursuit of a community's flourishing in a spirit of worship and prayer. Smart compassion holds together justice and evangelism, wisdom and revelation, and the broadly communal and deeply personal aspects of life. Smart compassion learns from a Nobel laureate's research on the return on investment of early childhood education and uses trustworthy data to measure effectiveness. It rejects the toxic "giver" and "receiver" posture of disempowering aid and starts from a strengths-based perspective. First and foremost, it never loses sight of Jesus as the Giver, Sustainer, and Redeemer of life and strives to maintain his posture in John 5:19: "I do what I see the Father doing" (my paraphrase).

What does compassion look like when the needs seem overwhelming? What is our role in the flourishing of our community? How does such work relate to worship? My hope is that this book encourages you to drag your piano into the street, even into death's valley, and to sing a new song of praise and supplication. But don't stop there. Gather some people of peace to join you in prayer, and learn all you can about how to create the best conditions possible for life to flourish. Then spend yourself well (Isaiah 58:10).

How?

This is the central question of this book. How do you spend yourself well? How do you collaborate with the Lord to see his kingdom come in your community as it is in heaven?

Even before we confidently identify our unique calling in life or get ourselves to a stable place where we feel competent to help others, we can make a life-altering difference for people in our community. As we do, we may find that the quest for a personalized calling diminishes in importance or becomes clarified in the process.

In this book we'll visit inspiring places and join thought-provoking conversations on how and where good and necessary change happens. A common thread you'll notice is the potential of *healing presence*, *radical hospitality*, and *collective empowerment*. When these three forces come together, you'll see new life. Through healing presence, we connect to people on a heart level and become conduits of God's presence and power. Through radical hospitality, we begin opening our homes and extending our family. And via collective empowerment, we'll know what's needed and will create conducive conditions for life to thrive. The work of smart compassion starts with drawing a circle around our community and saying, "It's going to be different in here!"

"Our" community is important. Collective ownership at stage one is essential. Smart compassion isn't doing for others what they can do themselves. It isn't a way for outsiders to provide better solutions for those less fortunate and unable to identify the real issues in their neighborhoods. Smart compassion draws from best practices in city renewal while remaining centered in the posture, "I do what I see the Father doing."

My hope for you is that in the face of personal struggles, limited time, complex needs, and endless options, you will develop a vision for how your community can thrive. I pray that you will gain confidence in distinguishing kind gestures from real change and that you and your congregation will experience greater levels of fullness and even healing as you step into the work of smart compassion.

All the stories in the book are true. Unless noted by quotation marks, people's real names are used. You can find more in-depth interviews with them at the City of Refuge website: SmartCompassion.net

As the journey unfolds, may God give you a vision for your community "as it is in heaven"!

1

When Doing Good Isn't Good Enough

One of Robin's earliest memories is being molested by her grandfather. The family faithfully attended church, yet there was a secret contained on the seventeenth pew, where they sat every Sunday for twelve years. "I grew up with my mom and grandparents. It was a weird, isolated, and lonely childhood. My grandfather was abusive throughout my childhood, but I didn't know it wasn't normal until much later," she says now, recounting vivid details with an eerie detachment. "My presence was my mother's worst nightmare and supposedly the reason she never did anything with her life," Robin recalls. "She reminded me of my inconvenient presence on a regular basis with her cutting words. I imagine she was molested by my grandpa as well. I don't think people can really have as much anger as she did for no reason."

"If only I had known!" is a common sentiment of many people who find out that they have been near those who suffer in silence. If only people in Robin's congregation had picked up on the warning signs. If only people had been aware of the prevalence and impact of early childhood trauma. If only . . .

The warning signs were definitely there. When she was young, Robin told strangers she wanted to live with them, and she acted out in class with highly destructive and inappropriate behavior. She was labeled as difficult, hyperactive, angry, and oversensitive. By the time she was thirteen, she had run away from home on numerous occasions.

Did you see someone like Robin this week? She is that one teenager who is always borrowing your daughter's clothes and never returning them. Perhaps you saw her hanging out at the park when you knew it was a school day. Maybe you'll see her walking around the mall on a Tuesday morning.

Knowledge makes a difference.

One of the greatest barriers hindering churches from making a significant impact in their communities is a lack of knowledge. It isn't apathy, insensitivity, or a lack of resources. When I work with a congregation that wants to engage with its community, I reveal local data that showcases needs in the neighborhood right around the church. The response from members is almost always, "We had no idea! If we had known, we would have responded differently."

I don't doubt it for a moment. Knowledge matters, and the good news is that knowledge has never been more accessible. In the time it takes you to read this introduction, you could learn the number of reports of human trafficking in your area, and could find out how your area compares to state and national averages on everything from teen births, sexually transmitted diseases, overdose deaths, access to primary and mental healthcare, and graduation rates to the number of children in poverty, single parenthood rates, crime indexes, housing problems, and much more.

For example, when you discover research like the landmark study of Adverse Childhood Experiences (ACE), which sheds light on the surprising prevalence of trauma in our homes, you learn that Robin's story, while it might seem rare, is actually commonplace. You learn that a congregation's inability to minister to her is a reflection of our difficulty in seeing what we're not looking for. When you are familiar with the research on adverse childhood experiences and the impact of one's biography on one's biology, your knowledge will help you identify and respond to children and families, especially those experiencing trauma.

In the pages that follow, we'll look at ways to overcome the knowledge gap. Knowledge really does make a difference.

Is more always better?

The idea that knowledge is required for smart compassion came from a string of failures. As a young pastor, my vision for our community in southern Florida was a bit like that of a high school student studying a foreign language: show up, get a good grade, but don't worry about actually gaining fluency. Participation points were enough; real change wasn't the goal. Unlike the highly motivated students in my high school who had recently emigrated from a Spanish-speaking country and were studying English, I lacked the vision, desperation, and immersion to become fluent in Spanish. Similarly, as a pastor, as long as I could say about our congregation, "We're showing up and our grades are good," I was pleased. I lacked the vision, desperation, and immersion to see real change in our community.

Then, in 2008, something dramatic happened: the economy tanked. Overnight, our city became the epicenter of the national recession. Life in Cape Coral, Florida—a city that became known for leading the nation in foreclosures—became almost eerie, and it happened really fast. Our beautiful coastal city, with more canals than any other city in the world, now looked as if it had been hit by the zombie apocalypse. I'd drive to work and see overgrown lawns and boarded-up homes almost everywhere I looked. I'd walk into a coffee shop that had always been buzzing with the energy of people laughing and talking, and it would be almost empty. Every day, in every office, the members of my congregation and I would listen to coworkers talk about job loss, relocation, or downsizing in some way or another. The city was enveloped by an inescapable and pervasive sadness. Unemployment and foreclosure rates were in a free fall. Crime, domestic violence, and overdose deaths were spiking, and on the cycle went.

We discovered a young homeless woman sleeping in our church. My brother mentored a boy for months before he learned the boy's family slept in their car in the parking lot of the local Walmart. Our city had no homeless shelter, and the needs were growing by the month.

What do you do in a place like this? I wasn't sure what our role as a church was in the community. Was housing now suddenly a part of our church's mission? To what degree should we expand our focus and commit ourselves to the flourishing of our community? I wasn't sure. Even if I had been sure, I wouldn't have known how we could make a real difference.

In the absence of knowledge, my strategy became "More is better." If we collected 25,000 pounds of food last year, let's try to collect 40,000 pounds this year: "C'mon church! Let's not let anyone go hungry!" Was food the most pressing need in our community? Sure. If someone asked, "What's your strategy for the food drive?" I'd say, "To help the food bank." If the person asked about the deeper challenges underlying our efforts, I'd say, "Let's not get too analytical; just put some extra cans in the cart." We generously and indiscriminately distributed resources, without much thought to measurements of success. Anecdotes of success were sufficient. In the absence of a real vision for change, all I needed were a couple of heartwarming stories to feel good about our efforts.

In addition to the "More is better" approach to community engagement, I leaned toward scalable, efficient, and transaction-oriented outreach programs, with priority given to those that could most directly translate into church growth. Food and clothing drives were perfect examples. They were easy, tangible, and scalable, and everyone could participate. My thought was: once we discover a need, we create a program to meet the need, and then people's gratitude will be a conveyor belt to a front-row seat on Sunday morning. My rationale might not have been quite that cavalier, but looking back, I'm amazed at how little thought I gave to the question of our role in the healing and flourishing of our community. We were good at "doing outreach," but we had no vision for real change.

Every detail . . . except one

A single event in 2008 rattled my perspective enough to make me go back to the drawing board and ask some basic questions about what to do in response to the increasing stresses and brokenness in our community.

Christmas was approaching, and a nearby school had a large number of children from families who were struggling to make ends meet. So our church decided to throw an elaborate Christmas party for these families. The idea started to snowball as we began to plan it. We might not have known how to create jobs, assist with housing, or help much with life-controlling addictions, but we could throw a good party! We raised a large amount of money for gifts and grocery cards, and we worked hard at all kinds of preparations. Then, on one December evening, we put on a red carpet event complete with a catered meal, theatrical performance, family pictures, gift bags, and customized presents for each child. We had carefully thought through every detail . . . except one.

How would this generous gift affect these families?

That night, it was a single encounter that changed everything for me. I was greeting people in our lobby toward the end of the party when two boys ran up to a couple of older women from our congregation. The little boys wrapped their arms around the women's legs and said, "Thank you! Thank you! How did you know?" They turned around to their father, who was standing off at a distance, and yelled, "Daddy! These are the women who bought us the presents!"

It was the look in his eyes that broke the whole event for me. That father was embarrassed, belittled at not being able to provide for his own kids. From the look on his face, he wanted to hide. But he had to show up for his kids to receive their gifts. His dignity was the price of admission. And he was willing to pay it.

I watched this man's reaction, and knew that embarrassment was exactly what I would feel if I were in his shoes. *What are we doing?!* I thought. Why hadn't we secretly given the presents to the parents to give to their children on Christmas? Or even better, why hadn't we let them buy presents at a reduced rate so that they had more options and more buy-in?

What we had done, I suddenly realized, was the equivalent of malpractice. Our hearts were in the right place, but my heart sank as I realized how misguided our efforts had been. We had based our response on reckless assumptions, no education, and no real willingness to assume the posture that true compassion requires. Had we really spent a ton of money only to cut off someone's dignity in an ill-advised attempt to "make a difference"?

Back to the drawing board

I walked away from that Christmas event dismayed by my own arrogance. I started to think about all the other projects we were involved in both as a church and a family. I began to stand back and consider if it really was a good thing to let our ten-year-old children serve food to homeless men and women. I had told myself for several years that children learn compassion and become less entitled by serving others. My heart had been in the right place, but I was beginning to realize how misguided my thinking was. Had I actually let the homeless become an object lesson for our kids?

In the wake of these changes in our community, our congregation went back to the drawing board. For us, the drawing board began with prayer. There was no strategizing at first. We gathered leaders of our congregation, and we began to pray this prayer: "God, give us your heart for your people, and help us see them as you see them. Teach us what we're supposed to do in this city."

We began to deconstruct everything we thought we knew. First, we began by getting rid of our assumption that we even had the first clue how to best help our community! We invited the church to join us for a forty-day period of prayer and fasting.

This time of brokenness, prayer, and fasting became the catalyst for the wonderful things that would come. We became more intentional in getting to know our community. We wanted to be more familiar with our own backyard than anyone else was. How did we do that?

Staff and volunteers from our congregation went to the people who had the closest contact with our community: educators, nonprofit leaders, police officers, emergency room nurses, and leaders of other churches. We approached these community leaders with two questions: "What's working well?" and "What's most needed?"

We discovered some hidden treasures in our city. There were churches and nonprofits running fantastic ministries that few people knew about. The need to "get the word out" about these services was one major theme of our conversations. One practical way we responded to this need was by creating a small resource guide. We distributed it everywhere in our community so that everyone would know where to turn for help when a crisis hit. We quickly distributed these little resource guides throughout the city—to police officers, grocery stores, banks, emergency rooms, local businesses, and individuals.

We also learned that clothing drives, food pantries, and church-run thrift stores dotted our city's landscape. Yet in our city of 170,000 people, there wasn't a single homeless shelter. Despite the exponential growth in opioid abuse, there was no inpatient drug and alcohol treatment center. Because there weren't enough approved foster homes in the city, most nights there were children sleeping in the offices of government social workers.

What do we do with this information in the church? I remember the first time I shared the information about kids in foster care sleeping in government buildings. I showed our congregation the specific ratio of the number of foster children to the number of licensed and active foster homes. I showed the foster care facility on a map and shared the stories of kids sleeping in social workers' offices in a government building for that week alone. I then drew a ten-mile radius around the office building and asked, "How many churches do you think are inside this radius?" There was a collective gasp in the room as little red dots suddenly lit up the map. Thirty-one churches within ten miles surrounded the building, and yet children facing unspeakable trauma were forced to sleep in offices.

Today, when I share this kind of information with congregations, the response to such jolting realities is always the same: *We had no idea!* We didn't either at first. The problem for our congregation wasn't our lack of concern. It wasn't even apathy. It was our lack of knowledge. We needed a clear vision and a smart strategy.

We needed to learn smart compassion.

One open door

In the early days of our work, I came across a story that captured the essence of the most important shift we needed to make. Just before sunset on a Friday evening in 1859, a man named Henri Dunant walked in utter dismay across the Italian countryside, surveying a fifteen-mile battlefield where forty thousand soldiers lay dead and dying. The Battle of Solferino was the most savage battle the country had ever seen.

Dunant stood in utter disbelief that so many wounded soldiers had been abandoned. The nearby townspeople had secluded themselves behind locked doors, waiting for the horrific sounds of the wounded to die down.

In a moment of outrage and desperation, Dunant ran through the streets rallying the townspeople, crying out, "All are brothers, all are brothers!" The people responded. They began to open their doors to the hurting and wounded soldiers. Before Saturday dawned, several makeshift hospitals were saving hundreds of lives. It was an amazing feat: on Friday night the townspeople hid inside their homes, unable to fathom the hell outside; on Saturday morning, a hope had exploded into action.

All of this began with one open door. It began with one person looking out and discovering that the "problem" was simply another human being in need!

Everyone who opened their door that night had every reason not to. Their apprehensions likely compounded exponentially as they thought through what-if scenarios. *What if they rob us? What if I catch a disease? What if there's a backlash for helping our enemies? I've heard those men are savages. Who knows? Maybe they're getting what they deserve. It's absolutely chaotic out there. I'm not good with blood. This house is a wreck. I've got a thousand things piling up here. If there's time later, I'll see what I can do.*

It takes a mix of compassion, selflessness, and boldness to sidestep all of those justifications and open your door. In Solferino, as neighbors began bringing food and supplies and blankets, caring for the wounded, and noticing others doing the same, they began to experience the energy and hope of *collective empowerment*. As they opened themselves and their homes to those in need, they drew near to the other through *radical hospitality*. Their close attention to the specific needs and areas that tilted the balance between life and death is a picture of *healing presence*.

It's often easier to close our doors. When our consciences nag us, we can toss out a few gifts to justify our separation from those in crisis. Opening our doors is a powerful first act.

When collective empowerment, radical hospitality, and healing presence come together, you'll always find new life. A Friday and Saturday in Italy changed battlefields forever. Dunant's prayer—his plea that all are siblings; all are family—changed modern history. Dunant's actions marked the beginning of what we know as the International Movement of the Red Cross and Red Crescent.

What about your community? How well do you know it? Is doing good no longer good enough? Do you have a vision for real change as you pray, "God, your kingdom here as it is in heaven"?

Let's draw a circle around our neighborhoods and say, "Things are going to be different here."

Let's start waging peace.

Let's open our front doors.

Let's get to work.

2

Compassion + Wisdom

A mother, "Stephanie," was staring into the open fridge as if a prepared meal was about to miraculously appear when the doorbell rang. A surge of anger caught her off guard to the point that she laughed as she approached the door.

There stood the caseworker, who had been sent to help her develop better communication and discipline techniques. This was part of a "diversion plan" to keep Stephanie's kids out of foster care. Stephanie was embarrassed and defensive about the whole arrangement.

So far Stephanie had tried to convey the idea that these services weren't necessary. Each week, she had cleaned the apartment, masked the strong smell of cigarette smoke, and politely engaged in their program. Not this night. Stephanie's kitchen was a disaster, her kids were hungry, and the smell of smoke was undeniable.

The trainer didn't seem fazed as she sat down at the kitchen table and slid aside some loose papers and dirty dishes to open her notebook. "So how'd the game go last week?" she asked.

So predictable, Stephanie thought. *Always a little small talk to soften things up.* "It was good. He did a good job," she said. As the conversation moved to parenting, Stephanie grew tense. Her mind ran from the kids in the back room to the looming question of dinner to her feelings about this trainer. She wondered what the trainer was thinking of her, and she thought about the thousand and one issues in her life that outranked the questions in this woman's notebook.

Finally, the polite and vague show had run its course. Stephanie interrupted the trainer mid-sentence. "Do you really want to know how to help me?" Stephanie said. She didn't wait for a response. "Why don't you help me clean this kitchen? That's what I need right now. I need a clean kitchen. Because these kids haven't eaten, and they don't know why you're here, and they don't know why their mom isn't cooking them dinner."

Stephanie didn't need to go any further. The trainer closed her notebook and stood up. "Where do you want to start? I can start with the dishes if you want to work on dinner."

What is compassion?

That night, there wasn't much conversation on healthy parenting attachment. But there was a clean kitchen, a good meal, and a little more trust than before. You can imagine that by dropping the agenda, closing the workbook, rolling up her sleeves, and listening to Stephanie's voice, the trainer expanded her potential for future influence on Stephanie's life. Principles like "Listen well before speaking" and "Conform the agenda to the person, not the person to the agenda" are important. But the relational posture we see here is what we need to focus on first.

The work of compassion doesn't begin with work. Compassion is a posture before an activity. Compassion isn't best thought of as a catch-all word for helpful service, good deeds, or kind actions. There are many ways to help people, and compassion is one of them, but it's best to distinguish the various avenues of service and aid.

Compassion means "to suffer with." Its Latin origin combines the preposition *com* (with) and *pati* (to suffer). In English, *passion* means "to suffer." It may be surprising to read that the word *passion* has anything to do with suffering. Modern understandings of passion have drifted quite far from the original meaning— although phrases like "I would die for . . ." may shed light on how we gravitated from that which we would suffer for to that which evokes heightened energy and commitment. In any case, the main thing is to recover the core meaning of *com-passion*.

When we think of the word *compassion*, the sacrificial love demonstrated in the passion of Christ—his death on the cross— is the right centering image. While many people might visualize participating in a community cleanup day or serving at the local homeless shelter when they think of compassion, it is Christ's work on the cross that holds the fullest meaning of the word. One of the earliest songs in the church captures Jesus' embodiment of compassion. Paul writes that Jesus,

> who, being in very nature God, did not consider equality with God something to be used to his own advantage; rather, he made himself nothing by taking the very nature of a servant, being made in human likeness. And being found in appearance as a man, he humbled himself by becoming obedient to death—even death on a cross! (Philippians 2:6-8)

This is compassion. And before we can say, "Yeah, well, that's Jesus! Lower the bar a tad," let's note that the apostle Paul leads into the song with these words in verse 5: "In your relationships with one another, *have the same mindset as Christ Jesus*" (emphasis mine).

The posture of compassion

Harper Lee, in her novel *To Kill a Mockingbird*, captures the posture of compassion well: "You never really understand a person until you consider things from his point of view—until you climb into his skin and walk around in it."[1]

Compassion connects people in a place of suffering with an undeterred bent toward life. A firefighter who spots a barely conscious person in a building on fire but isn't willing to enter the building isn't much help. A firefighter willing to enter the building but who doesn't know how to escape burning buildings isn't much help either. Compassion does both: it is willing to jump in, and it also knows how to emerge from ground zero. Compassion is up close (*proximity*), on level ground (*solidarity*), and deeply connected to the other's perspective and feelings (*emotional connectedness*), with a perspective that is always oriented toward truth and life.

Proximity, solidarity, and emotional connectedness are essential qualities of compassion's posture. Let's look briefly at these three qualities and how Stephanie's caseworker embodied them.

Proximity

We can feel sympathy for a person from a distance, but compassion only happens when we draw close. It's forged in the intricate connection between people. The caseworker could feel sorry for Stephanie after reading her file. But only in her presence could compassion be birthed.

Solidarity

As we take a seat next to others on level ground and meet them where they're at, we reject both the higher ground of judge and the lower ground of victim. Romans 12:15 summarizes it: "Rejoice with those who rejoice; mourn with those who mourn." Be where they are. Whether they are on an ash heap or a mountaintop, strive to be fully present with them and their feelings. The caseworker's attentiveness to Stephanie's needs and her willingness to set aside her agenda is a picture of solidarity.

Emotional connectedness

We tend to the heart and not just the mind and circumstances. We view all human life as sacred and eternal, and we're sensitive to the ways people are dehumanized and lose their voice and sense of identity. Material improvements are essential, but they fail to touch the depths of Jesus' invitation to life and freedom. The caseworker's desire to hear Stephanie's story and connect on a heart level is a step toward emotional connectedness.

What is smart compassion?

In the same way that compassion changes an individual, smart compassion changes a community. Smart compassion remains compassionate as it scales. It doesn't become less human, less responsive, or less connected. It doesn't leave the ground, abandon the nuances of individuals and families in a specific community, or disempower people by relating to them as mere recipients of services. Smart compassion is, put simply, ten thousand acts of authentic compassion that are strategic, well networked, and responsive to the real needs of a defined community. The prayers and collaborative research of community members help establish a clear vision for their community's flourishing. Strategies and measurements rise from this work and align clearly with the vision. Traditional recipients of services become researchers, designers, and directors of those services. Programs derive from local relationships and are always steps toward the realization of a vision, which emerges from within the community.

When you listen to appeals to collect food for local food banks but hear nothing of job training and decide to ask "But why?" and "Is it working?" from a posture of compassion and a willingness to pursue a vision for real change, you're taking a step toward smart compassion. When you see opioid abuse in your community and decide that it's not enough to throw money at the problem or sit with people in their suffering, and so begin to pursue a vision to end the epidemic, you're taking steps toward smart compassion. When compassion is an integral part of your life and you pray continually for God's revelation for your community and pursue wisdom for what really works, you're on the doorstep of smart compassion.

Compassion is smart when it digs deeper and penetrates the soil nutrients and toxins that create and constrain life. When first responders are continually called out to the same area and for the same circumstance, the underlying causes must be addressed and transformed. In our congregational context in 2008, compassion would have led us to replace the Christmas party with more relational and empowering connections with people. Smart compassion would have led us to ask, "How do we help eradicate homelessness in our city and help those who are addicted to drugs or alcohol experience recovery and wholeness in Jesus?"

When we follow Jesus, we end up on the margins. It just happens. Like the natural pull of gravity, the way of Jesus leads toward redeeming brokenness in the belly of the beast. The way of Jesus isn't the creation of an oasis and big signs for those to see it from far away. The way of Jesus means rolling up your sleeves and jumping into the middle of life with people. The way of Jesus means working within the local church, which is the best equipped, most uniquely positioned, and most internally motivated group of people to heal and invigorate communities. God brings dead things back to life!

What is the broader story?

Say your church is just down the street from Stephanie's apartment. One evening you see her sitting outside her door, smoking a ciga-rette and quietly crying. You're on your way to a church committee meeting, but you decide to go over and check on her. She is willing to talk, and you decide to forgo the meeting. You learn that she relapsed last week and failed a drug test, and the earliest she can get her kids back is after a minimum of five months of separation. This is a crushing setback after months of progress.

How do you respond? Stephanie is devastated and angry. She blames others and hates herself. Most concerning, though, is the sense of powerlessness in her voice. How do you help? Does the moment call for a motivational speech to reinvigorate that fiery and indomitable spirit? Just a listening ear and time to vent?

Let's take a seat next to Stephanie outside her door and look closely at her family's situation and neighborhood characteristics. Just over a year ago, Stephanie was a bartender with one main rule at work: Never give out your number. She already had one failed marriage and a young son and was all too familiar with the vortex into which single parents without good job prospects can fall. Some 70 percent of the households in her neighborhood were caught in this vortex.

Of course, she believes her current boyfriend, Kevin, is different. For one, he was extremely persistent. When they first met, he was at the bar with some friends to watch the NBA finals, but his full attention was on her. They spoke casually for the first half hour or so. Later, after his friends had left and most everyone at the bar had cleared out, he stood up, motioned to the side of the bar, and said with a coy grin, "Come here for a minute." She stopped cleaning and walked over to him. When they faced each other, unobstructed for the first time, he grabbed her hand playfully and said, "I'd really like to take you to dinner one night. What do you say?"

Stephanie was only twenty-three, but she wasn't one to get lost in a moment like this anymore. She pulled her hand back and smiled, "Sorry, I don't date people I meet at a bar."

"Okay, let's imagine we're not at your bar," Kevin persisted. "Say we're coworkers at my office instead. I'd still ask you to dinner. Thursday night . . . c'mon, you never know."

Stephanie had relented. Now, a year later, they're a fragile family of four living in a five-hundred-square-foot apartment surrounded by stats that warn of a difficult road ahead.

Between Stephanie's biological parents, there had been eleven spouses/paramours/longtime boyfriends and girlfriends, and Stephanie hadn't spent more than a few months at a time with any of them. Kevin is the youngest of four boys raised by a single mother. Stephanie reminds him of his mom; they are both thick-skinned survivors bent on protecting their kids from the chaos they endured as children. Kevin is gentle and fun and, in Stephanie's words, "A big friendly blob." Despite his persistence when they first met, these days he has no backbone, no initiative. She tries to push and motivate him, but there's nothing to latch onto. He describes it differently. He says, "I'm just not made to play house all the time, and her intensity is suffocating."

A year into their relationship, their pattern is fairly well established: a few weeks of stability followed by some major derailment. These lapses—whether it is Kevin not coming home one evening because of his drug addiction or spending the few extra dollars they have on lunch or drinks—trigger a deep rage in Stephanie. She has tried to be so careful with men. The more she recites the unkept promises he made to her that lowered her defenses, the deeper her rage grows.

So much of Stephanie's energy—she says "every fiber in my being"—is set on *not* repeating the mistakes of her biological mother. Yet it is as if there is a constant, unrelenting magnet that pulls her in the same direction.

This is where the story gets a bit uncomfortable and complicated. It would be easy, and maybe tempting, to look exclusively at Stephanie as an individual disconnected from a family system and community.

This line of thinking goes something like, "Our choices establish our trajectory, and the quality of our choices determines our outcomes." Yet when you look closely at the neighborhood in which Stephanie lives, there seems to be more at play than good and bad choices.

Stephanie's income (just below the federal poverty line), family structure (single parent, cohabitating), education level (high school diploma), job sector (service), and home address growing up (row house, a few streets down) are similar to the attributes of many of her neighbors. Why? Why is one's zip code a greater predictor of health and life expectancy than one's genetic code?

If Stephanie's sons follow national trends, there's a greater than 45 percent chance that they too will live beneath the poverty line. Her boys aren't alone. They represent more than one out of every five kids in the United States. Think about that for a moment. In the United States, 22 percent of kids live below the federal poverty line—that's $24,000 for a family of four in 2015. The number of kids in poverty is greater than the population of the fifth most populous U.S. state. Some 40 percent of these kids will remain in poverty throughout their adult lives. Child poverty rates in the United States are among the highest of any developed country, ranking just below Mexico. These are solid, indisputable numbers that should grip all of us and demand we do better for our kids.

A friend recently told me of his daughter's trip to a country in the Majority World, where she encountered extreme childhood poverty for the first time. When she returned, she asked her father, "What are we doing to eliminate childhood poverty in our own backyard?" My friend stumbled around for a bit and then shared about a few outreach efforts in the area. His daughter then asked, "Is it working?"

He admitted it wasn't. Then she said, "Dad, I think we can do better."

If we could hear the aspirations of the sixteen million boys and girls who are presently living below the federal poverty line, we would move heaven and earth to change this reality.

The question is, how?

What's the broader story of which Stephanie is a part? How might smart compassion get to the root of the forces shaping her quality of life and transform her life through Christ? What does compassion mean for these shared obstacles in struggling communities?

When a community's water supply is contaminated, we cannot simply treat an individual's symptoms or just give people in-home filters. We must address the issues at their roots as well. If there's lead in the water because the pipes are corroded, at some point you have to replace the pipes. If a high percentage of young mothers are struggling with childcare and low-wage jobs, it makes sense to start programs for these families, not just sit with them as they suffer the lack of opportunity.

For our compassion to be smart, we must recognize the porous nature of our lives. We're part of a larger ecosystem. We're part of family systems and broader cultures and social structures that give shape to our lives. When these systems and structures are warped, compassion must manifest itself in more than assistance to cope with the deformed shapes.

We must look, all at once, from a micro to a mezzo to a macro level. All of these levels of cultural influence affect our lives as we affect them. Winston Churchill once said, "We shape our buildings; thereafter, they shape us." The same is true for the larger structures and systems we live within.

In this book, we will distinguish three levels of connection with people, and the posture that best corresponds with them. Each part of this book explores one of these levels, which can be seen as concentric circles that go from micro to mezzo to macro level.

Healing presence on the personal (micro) level is the act of connecting with another at the deep and vulnerable places where our identity, relationships, drives, fears, and hopes are forged.

Radical hospitality on the family (mezzo) level is the work of opening our homes and extending our family to strangers.

Collective empowerment on the community (macro) level is the work of rightly placed doors and nets.

Let's examine each of these in a bit more detail. We'll start with the larger picture of communities and systems, zoom in to homes, and then move to the more intimate personal level.

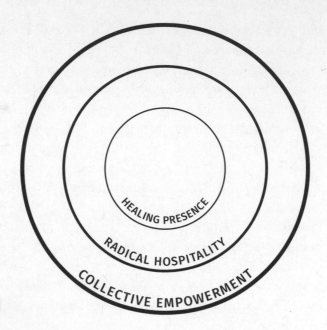

Collective empowerment: Community level

Collective empowerment is the work of rightly placed doors and nets. People need safe places to land and opportunities and empowerment to flourish. We need to resist all forms of aid that perpetuate cycles of dependency. You have unique knowledge, resources, connections, and abilities that can open unseen doors and facilitate unexpected breakthroughs for people who need them.

On this broader level, the scope and complexity of needs can overwhelm us and have a canceling-out effect. At the outset, we simply need to be willing to stop in our tracks on the way to the committee meeting, sit with someone else's reality, and commit to changing our understanding of what constitutes "church work." There's power in simply committing to a community's flourishing. There's power in saying, "I'm not going to bury my head or find convenient narratives to justify my indifference or lack of engagement." There's power in halting fatalistic and ambivalent reactions. We lean in, we learn, we hope, we open ourselves to vulnerability, and mainly, we spend ourselves well on behalf of others.

It takes a certain level of verve to run through the streets of a shell-shocked, fearful community, surrounded by carnage, shouting, "All are brothers!" as Dunant did. The good news is that when you're drawn into a compelling *why*, the *how*s will find their place in time. First, we must draw a circle and get to work.

Imagine the change when the church draws a circle around a community and says, "It's going to be different in here! We will know this community. We will know the needs. We will know the resources. We will pray and work continually to see God's kingdom here as it is in heaven. We will care for people who aren't looking to be cared for and ensure that people know where to turn for help when a crisis hits." When churches draw such a circle, it's a game changer.

To move toward collective empowerment, we need to identify areas of need and areas of opportunity and wisely align resources to meet them collectively. What are the prevailing risk factors that need to be addressed? What are the protective factors that need to be expanded, improved upon, and communicated more broadly or clearly? These are areas we'll unpack in part 3 of this book, which focuses on collective empowerment.

For example, say you learn that adolescents in your community commit the vast majority of crimes between two thirty in the afternoon and six in the evening, and that there's only one after-school program in an area with over 9,300 high school students. A lot of teenagers loitering around town after school is a risk factor for your community. You can obtain this information in a single afternoon. You can also obtain information about effective programs from Blueprints for Healthy Youth Development, which provides a registry of evidence-based programs that are proven to work well, including the Eisenhower Foundation's Quantum Opportunities Program and the Big Brothers Big Sisters program.[2] Knowledge about what works well—and what doesn't—is crucial. For example, less than 5 percent of the programs that Blueprints reviews are designated as model programs. Knowledge has never been more accessible for the pursuit of smart compassion.

Thinking "doors and nets" is helpful for visualizing collective empowerment. Make sure there's a safe place for people to land when they need it, but never disempower people by doing for them what they can do themselves. There may be doors you can open that people like Stephanie can't access or even see. If you can't help her in tangible ways, you probably know some people who can. You may also need to knock down a wall occasionally and create a door. Practically, the distinction here is between assisting Stephanie personally—perhaps giving her some cash to keep the lights on—and opening an employment agency to help people in Stephanie's neighborhood.

Switch to agricultural imagery, and collective empowerment means you're attending to the soil nutrients and toxins that create and constrain life. Life is God's work, and we collaborate with God as stewards as best we can. We give witness to (evangelize about) the source of life—the triune God—and we steward resources toward optimal conditions for life to flourish.

Radical hospitality: Household level

On the household level, we need radical hospitality. For some people, we don't just open doors; we open our homes and our hearts. We offer the gift of extended family and attune ourselves to the highly specific and sublimely mundane acts of love that can forever change generations. There are many future brothers, sisters, mothers, fathers, daughters, and sons who would love to be grafted into your family. You can't do it for all of them, but you can do it for some. Give those who are lonely and struggling space around the table on holidays, include them in family picnics and ball games, and find other simple ways to share life with them.

Some new friends of ours went kayaking one late afternoon and parked a car where they planned to exit the river. But they forgot their keys in the car parked at the point of entry. This family of five was stuck on the side of a river at nine thirty at night, in the middle of nowhere, with a dying cell phone. They had been in town for all of four days, and we were the only people they knew to call for help. When I answered their call, the guy said, "Oh my goodness, I'm *so* glad you picked up the phone."

The call came in under their name. If it was a random number, I likely wouldn't have answered. Radical hospitality leads us to move some folks, who might normally be just a number, into our closer list of contacts. Perhaps some will even break into the "favorites" list.

When you have a rich, responsive, and supportive network, it may be easy to overlook the need for radical hospitality. But when you're stuck and you're not even sure who can help, you get it. Nothing can replace the gift of a soft place to land and a person who will answer the door.

Radical hospitality is an area where we may need to learn from other cultures. People who live in societies that emphasize autonomy over community often struggle with the inconvenience and vulnerability hospitality requires. When you invite people into your life and home, it gets messy. There's no way around it. You learn all sorts of things about yourself very quickly. But it's a good kind of messy, and it stretches us in phenomenal ways. Things we accept as givens about ourselves and our culture can actually change. Hospitality is a cultural practice, and because it's uncommon in our culture, we will need to practice it until it begins to feel more natural. And hopefully, it will become more commonplace.

A community-oriented perspective that makes it normal rather than an anomaly to have houseguests for dinner may look weird from a hyperindividualistic perspective. But this perspective is certainly more biblical than one that considers the home a private sphere. Who's to say you can't be inconvenienced in your own home? Think of your home as a haven, but one not limited to your nuclear family. There's no better way to teach your children compassion than radical hospitality.

It's true: what one person may call "hospitality" another may call a "lack of boundaries." Radical hospitality requires a mind-set shift. "What night this week can we have that single mother and her kids we met down the street over for dinner?" "Thanksgiving is next week; who needs a place to go?" You may need to cook a little more food, or leave some space open in your home, or spend a little more on groceries—but these things will reap dividends far beyond what you can imagine.

When a church practices radical hospitality together, it gains a reputation in the community as a place to turn for help in crisis. In Denver, Colorado, Sharon Ford did some simple math. In the United States, there were 300,000 churches and 130,000 kids needing a family. She thought, "If each church just takes one child, the problem is solved." Thanks to the program she helped launch, Wait No More, Colorado saw the number of children awaiting adoption drop by half in one year! The program has been expanded to several states across the country. Like the program Safe Families, which provides a much-needed relational support structure for families *before* a court intervention, Wait No More helps position churches to have a collective and deeply personal impact in their communities.

Part 2 of this book goes into more depth about what radical hospitality looks like at the household level.

Healing presence: Individual level

On a personal level, we need healing presence. This is where the deeper, heart-level connection happens. Here's an absolutely extraordinary thought that becomes an even more extraordinary reality when we experience it: we can become conduits of God's very presence and power to others. Offering healing presence to others means recognizing God's sovereignty over every aspect of life, being aware of God's presence, and striking a posture of dependence on God's leading. When I believe that God is sovereign, present, and at work, it changes my responsibility in some pretty drastic ways. I don't need to fall into a practical agnosticism and become a "fix it" man. The Holy Spirit is with us. God is with us! Jesus captured the posture well: "I in them and you in me—so that they may be brought to complete unity. Then the world will know that you sent me and have loved them even as you have loved me" (John 17:23).

So many people suppress pain and shame because they don't believe real healing is possible. For them, coping with life seems more realistic than actual freedom. I was such a person before my wife and I began our healing journey. A counselor who incorporated healing prayer into his practice once read to me a single verse, Hebrews 12:15: "See to it that no one falls short of the grace of God and that no bitter root grows up to cause trouble and defile many." The counselor then said to me something like, "Judgments follow the laws of sowing and reaping. They become bitter roots and they need to be pulled up. You're right to forgive those who've sinned against you, but you also need to repent of your judgments about them. Can you see how they're becoming bitter roots?" My mind flooded with new connections between past hurts and present bitter roots. The counselor led me through a time of prayer that opened my soul to grace where unacknowledged judgments had been wreaking havoc. His knowledge of God's Word, understanding of the pathways of redemption, and receptivity to the Holy Spirit were incredible gifts to me and my marriage.

Have you ever experienced such a gift of actual freedom from sin and brokenness? Has someone helped you connect on a heart level with the living God? There's no substitute for the transformation that God can bring to the depths of a human soul. It's why the metaphor of new birth is used in the New Testament. God can make all things new! Sometimes we simply settle for far less than God is willing to give us.

Imagine the gift such a connection would be for Stephanie. An employment agency can help her break cycles of dependency and heartache. Radical hospitality can provide much-needed community and friendship. But only God can breathe new life into her soul. Life is God's work and God's gift. When we press into this space of prayer and tangible redemption with others, this space where the subterranean plates shift, we see some truly miraculous changes. Part 1 of *Smart Compassion* unpacks the gifts of healing presence.

Compassion is birthed in suffering well

Before we begin part 1, however, let's pause for a moment to consider the way that smart compassion is birthed. The first work of smart compassion at all of these levels—healing presence, radical hospitality, and collective empowerment—is connecting with another in that person's suffering. But you can't do that unless you've learned to suffer well yourself.

How comfortable are you sitting on the ash heap with someone who is suffering? How comfortable are you taking a seat next to Stephanie on her stoop, listening to her story, and sitting with her tears? Are such feelings strangers to you? Have you ever sat like this yourself? Have you ever slumped outside your own door, with your face toward the pavement? Have you ever doubted whether you'll recover?

It's not that we need to be able to say to every person we encounter, "I know exactly what you're going through." The ability to relate to another's feelings certainly helps, and when you've experienced redemption in a similar place, it can help a great deal. But you can extend compassion even if you've never gone through similar life experiences. The only deal breaker here is the refusal to connect on an emotional level.

Leanne Payne, one of my favorite teachers of the practice of healing prayer, describes this inability to connect with others on an emotional level as a "head-heart schism." When we live out of our heads and refuse to feel emotions, and that refusal becomes a way of life, connecting with people in their suffering becomes impossible. Conversely, when our heads and hearts are connected and we allow God to excavate our own souls in times of suffering and adversity, we're poised to meet others there as well.

Several years ago, Bonnie and I walked through a painful time in our marriage. We had lost a child in the third trimester, and neither of us responded to it well. Our problems were there before Addison's death, but at the loss of our baby, the lid came off. One scary afternoon, I was driving to nowhere, completely disillusioned and contemplating all sorts of terrible ideas. An image came to my mind of a battlefield strewn with buried land mines. It was as though God was downloading this image and saying to me, "Just so you know, here's where you're at right now." A spirit of rebellion, fatalism, resentment, flesh desires, and well-masked fears mixed together in a soothing, toxic cocktail. The longer I sipped it, the more likely I was to make some really bad mistakes.

Fortunately, I had a good friend who embodied qualities of smart compassion. When I called Brad, he stopped everything and drove across the state to meet with me. He must have thought I was crazy at first. (I now like to say that it wasn't really me; it was a foreign and sinister imposter of me who had temporarily grabbed the steering wheel.) The good news is that my crazy talk and rawness of emotions didn't send Brad running to the hills or reaching for the gavel. His presence was peaceful and steadying. For a day and a half, he paused his life to take a seat on the ash heap next to me and make sure that life rather than death came from it.

The posture of compassion requires long-suffering in uncomfortable places. You have to create a safe space for authenticity. Brad affirmed what he could and sat with me as I talked in circles. He was smart: he didn't feed into my warped perspective by saying, "Yeah, you're right. That's awful. Let me pat you on the back as you plunge headlong over that cliff." He also never asked questions like, "What are your deepest desires?" But he was compassionate, so neither did he cut me off with, "You just need to go back and fix this right now." He affirmed what he could and didn't validate my accusations or bitterness.

Instead, after listening to my long diatribe of accusations and judgments, Brad said, "It's hard to forgive, isn't it?" There was authenticity in his empathy. But the focus on forgiveness oriented me toward life. The more I vented, the closer I came to the real and deeper issues. I recognized certain truths and lies that I hadn't been aware of. Fortunately, Brad didn't shortchange this process. If his focus had been only on truth, and correcting my deviations from it, I never would have gotten to the deeper issues beneath my struggle with conflict.

Soon I regained my bearings, and Bonnie and I were able to walk through a healing journey that made our marriage stronger than it had ever been. Brad's gift of compassion will forever reap dividends.

To become a wounded healer

The specifics of smart compassion are different for all of us. Our backgrounds, contexts, gifting, resources, relationships, and interests are all part of what we bring to the work of smart compassion. As we seek God's revelation and wisdom to see his vision for our community and the ways we can best make a difference, the picture will become clearer.

Stephanie did indeed lose her kids for a time, but she got them back, and is now a caseworker herself. She wouldn't use this language, but she's clearly a conduit of God's healing presence. She knows the look and sound of despair. She knows when it's time to close the notebook and roll up her sleeves. She knows how to match but not exceed people's effort, and she will move heaven and earth to open the right doors for her families. She's been there. And she's been *through* there, which means a great deal when you're in the thick of it and you can't see a way out.

We begin this journey of smart compassion by looking at healing presence: this initial work of seeing and responding to where God is already at work. Let's look first at how the realization of God's sovereignty and the awareness of God's presence suddenly pull the background of life onto the main stage.

HEALING PRESENCE

RADICAL HOSPITALITY

COLLECTIVE EMPOWERMENT

Part I

Healing Presence: Become a Conduit of God's Love

3

The Background Moves to the Foreground

The instructions are straightforward: spend two hours in a neighborhood and be fully present to God and the people you meet. The whole idea makes me nervous. I lean over to the older woman sitting next to me, "Sorry, I don't understand what that means," I whisper. "Is this some kind of a door-to-door evangelism campaign?"

She smiles. "Not really," she says. "But if that's where God leads you, go for it!"

Unlikely.

About fifty of us are gathered in a traditional church sanctuary on a Tuesday morning, preparing to split up into groups of three or four for two hours of "being fully present." The description is pretty loosey-goosey, but I seem to be the only one grasping for more details.

Our presenter, a charismatic guy in his late twenties wearing shorts, a T-shirt, and flip-flops, shares some logistics. Then he says, "If this is your first time, just remember four things: Love. Listen. Discern. Respond. That's what this is about. We want to show God's love to people in any way we can. We want to listen well to the Holy Spirit and the people we meet. We want to discern where God might be at work, and we want to respond to the Spirit's leading."[1]

After a short prayer, we meet up in our groups and drive to our assigned neighborhoods. I am with two middle-aged white women and one older African American man. They have all been part of these neighborhood prayer walks before. Jackie is a Lutheran, Renita is Pentecostal, and Russ attends a nondenominational, evangelical church. I am the nervous Mennonite guy who asks a lot of questions.

Our car ride conversation is intriguing. "So we're headed to a neighborhood near a college campus," I say. "And what exactly are we supposed to do there?"

Jackie, who exudes a gentle warmth, says, "We just walk and pray for the area. We pray for the homes and the people we see. We ask God to show us if there is something we're supposed to do. Don't strive too hard. Just be open."

This constant emphasis on "openness" puzzles me. "Just be receptive," they keep saying. But what does that *mean*? I prefer clear goals, tight schedules, objective feedback. It looks as though this is going to be some kind of exposure therapy.

Russ laughs and hits me in the arm. "You're good! Take a deep breath. You might be surprised what God does. This is my eighth time joining these neighborhood prayer walks, and I've seen God do some extraordinary things."

I try to put aside my skepticism. "Like what?" I ask.

"Well, a few weeks ago, I was with a prayer group that had two teenagers in it," Russ says. "As we drove past a home, one of the teenagers said, 'We need to go to that house. I think there's been a death in the family, and they're really hurting right now.'"

Russ raises his eyebrows to show how baffled he and the other adults had been. "'What?! C'mon,' I said to him. But we pulled around and stopped at the house. Sure enough, an older couple opened the door, and they were grieving deeply over the loss of a family member."

"That's crazy!" I say to Russ.

He shrugs his shoulders. "Not uncommon. You'll hear stories like that when we get back to the church this afternoon."

We pull into a parking spot, and my heart starts racing. I feel a bit embarrassed at my level of anxiety. Right away, I see a young guy walking toward us down a sidewalk on the other side of the road. *Oh, should I go speak with him?* I wonder. *No, just relax,* I think. Then I smile as the strangeness of this whole experience becomes apparent. Never before have I wondered if I should initiate a conversation with a stranger "just because." My mind races as it tries to make sense of what is happening.

We approach a Jewish temple and Jackie says, "Let's go and see if we can pray for the staff." The presenter had mentioned the need to pray for places of worship in the area. An older woman answers the door and Jackie says, "We're in the area to pray for the neighborhood, and we're curious if there are some things you'd like us to pray about."

The woman is clearly caught off guard and stumbles for a response. She finally says, "I've worked here for more than twenty years and this is a first!"

She smiles. "Hmm, well, you can definitely pray for this neighborhood. It's really gone downhill over the years. That's why we keep the doors locked." After a few minutes of conversation, she begins to warm up and invites us into her office. She shares about a few personal struggles and asks for prayer for some broken relationships. After the prayer, she has tears running down her cheek. "Thank you! That was a nice surprise."

We leave, and I think, *Not so bad. Nothing earth-shattering, but nothing cringe-worthy either.*

Next, we come across a young couple sitting on the steps of their front porch and smoking cigarettes. A newborn sleeps in a stroller beside them. I walk up, introduce myself, and repeat Jackie's line. "We're just in the area, praying for the neighborhood. Is there any way we can pray for you?"

The guy laughs and looks over to his girlfriend, who appears to be about seventeen years old. She doesn't smile back and puts her head down.

His smile disappears. "Well . . . I just got out of prison and need a job and a place to live. And . . ." His voice trails off as he looks back over at his girlfriend. "Probably some new friends. You know, just a lot of new stuff."

His openness to conversation is surprising, and we end up spending more than an hour with this couple. Russ, who lives close by, offers to meet with the young man the next week and help with his job search. Russ has a close friend who hires men recently released from prison, and he thinks his friend will give this young man a chance. Russ and the young father exchange numbers, and we pray together.

It is about time to head back to the church when I realize that none of my fears have played out. There has been one mildly awkward conversation with an agnostic college student, but even that brief encounter had some signs of life. The conversation with the young couple may have been a divine appointment. Some potential breakthroughs are definitely on the horizon for them, and Russ will be a great person to stay in contact with them.

When we return to the church, John, the friend I have come with, is busy helping a visibly intoxicated man park his bike in the parking lot. John's group had been sitting in a park across the street, praying, when they saw the guy fall off his bike. "Guess that's our divine appointment for the day," one of them said, and John ran over to help the man.

After a long conversation, John asked him, "So, where are you at? Fun? Fun with problems? Or just problems?" The man didn't say anything at first. Finally, he said, "No, there's nothing good anymore."

The prayer group brought him back to the church, hoping someone there would be able to help. Sure enough, one guy in long-term recovery and now active in recovery work himself is able to get the man into detox that day and walks with him through the process. A few weeks later, the man will be baptized at the church. With tears running down his cheek, he will thank God for new life and "a couple of angels sent to help wake me up."

Two hours. That's all. Story after story: some miraculous, most mundane, but all oriented toward new life.

Later that night, at the Indianapolis airport on my way home, I look around me and wonder: What would it be like to live fully present to God and the people around me? What would I see and experience that I miss right now? Is God really *that* present in our daily affairs? Am I just too preoccupied or self-absorbed to notice?

When the background emerges onto the main stage

Healing presence begins with an awareness of God's presence and power in our daily lives and interpersonal relationships. God is present! God is sovereign! God is faithful! God is good! God still speaks and heals! We are invited to collaborate with God in his ever-present redemptive work around us. Jesus' last words to the disciples as he sent them out with the great commission were, "And surely *I am with you* always" (Matthew 28:20, emphasis mine). Earlier, Jesus explained his own work as grounded in intimacy with the Father: "I do what I see the Father doing" (John 5:19, my paraphrase).

The realization of God's sovereignty and presence moves the background of life into the foreground. I think of Joshua Bell's violin experiment in a subway station in Washington, D.C., where he pulled out his multimillion-dollar Stradivarius and left his case open for tips. Bell, a world-famous violinist, played the same songs people had paid top dollar to hear the night before. No one noticed. No one recognized him. Everyone knows you don't see one of the best violinists in the world playing a priceless Stradivarius in a subway station! A few people tossed in some loose change or dollar bills as they passed by, probably out of a mild and highly ironic pity: *Here you go, buddy, get yourself a sandwich.* Who knows? Maybe he could trade up from that old violin one day.

Except for one woman. There was one woman in that subway station who had attended his concert the night before and recognized him. She stopped in utter disbelief. "Joshua Bell in a D.C. subway station?" Wherever she was going, it could wait. She could catch the next train.

Maybe the difference between this woman and everyone else that morning speaks to my struggle with being fully present. Too often I haven't lived with an expectation that God's presence would permeate my daily rhythms and interactions. For the two hours of that prayer walk, the background came alive. People and place were not merely part of the backdrop; they were part of the play itself. And life suddenly became a whole lot richer and fuller.

A strange paradox came along with this sudden awakening to the background of life. I had spent a couple of years trying to ignore the background of life and gain a sharper focus with my time and attention. My sensory spotlight was too diffuse and needed to narrow. Time management trainings and a myriad of books and seminars on productivity had instilled in me a relentless need to concentrate on what was most important. It wasn't easy, but I had learned to block out my surroundings and concentrate my attention.

But was the virtue now a vice? Had I taken the pursuit of concentration too far? The more I thought about it, the more I realized that the problem lay in where my concentration centered. Our concentration is largely determined by the stories we tell and the beliefs that underlie them. In my story, godlike things were everywhere. But God himself was not the center of my concentration. I had probably lived countless versions of the good Samaritan story, in which I was in full pursuit of godlike activities with God-ordained ones all around and in my rearview mirror.

Isaiah 26:3 is instructive here: "You will keep in perfect peace those whose minds are steadfast, because they trust in you." My unspoken paraphrase of this verse would have been something like: "I'll achieve peace as long as I keep my mind on the right things, including the things of God, because I don't trust in much outside myself." Strangely, God himself was always one step removed. Godlike things were everywhere . . . and I was in the center.

Lessons from the world of improv

Later, I found help with bringing the background of life more into the foreground in a surprising place: improv. My real need was to learn to be fully present to God and people in the moment and to eliminate the hurry, mental preoccupation, anxiety, and general self-absorption that characterized much of my daily life. Surprisingly, the principles of improvisational comedy helped cultivate this attentiveness to the present moment.

Good improvisation requires you to be a great student of the environment. You must first read the room and be fully attentive to your scene partner. There's no script to fall back on, so you've got to listen really well and go with what you receive. It's never "No;" it's always "Yes, and . . ." This is the scary part. You've got to fill in the space and take it somewhere. It may crash and fall flat. It may lead to unexpected brilliance. Either way, it's impossible to predict at the outset, and that's part of the fun. You never know what's going to happen.

Fortunately, the more you do it, the more comfortable it becomes. You learn to listen better and to become fully attuned to the person with whom you share the stage. Your responses become less awkward and predictable. The empty spaces that were once so scary now become the very places where some of the best things emerge. A playfulness softens rigidity; it's okay for everything not to be preprogrammed and highly controlled. Also, in an unexpected way, you learn to find and trust your voice because you're not locked to a script or specific role to play.[2]

The more I reflected on my short neighborhood prayer walk, the more it appeared to be an entirely different way to live. If God is present and at work in ways that transcend my "script," I should try to be fully present, try to accept inconveniences and everyday encounters. If this two-hour experiment was any indication, it would be a fuller, more fruitful, and more enjoyable way to live. I would need to soften the rigidity of my schedule, slow the pace a bit, and learn to attune myself to the Holy Spirit's promptings.

That night in the airport, while standing in a long line at Starbucks, I prayed, "God, help me to live fully present to you and the people around me." For the next few months, I would try to extend this two-hour experiment into a way of life by focusing my attention on God and learning to cultivate those four practices: Love. Listen. Discern. Respond. These four practices, when we put them together, enable us to become a healing presence in our communities.

In chapter 3, we'll look at love; in chapter 4, we'll examine listening; and in chapter 5, we'll set our attention to discerning and responding. But first, let's explore the blocks we sometimes face on the way to becoming a healing presence.

I'll just add healing presence to my already frenetic life

At first, the effort of extending this short experiment into a way of life was a bit like a Manhattan banker who takes a weekend trip to the country, becomes enamored of rural life, and decides to become a farmer in his spare time. Adding a completely different way of life on top of an already full and frenetic one, without modifications, wasn't realistic. I thought I could simply add, "Be fully present to God and people" on top of the instructions I was already following: "Be as productive as possible" and "Never let anyone down." My attempts to graft one way of living onto another reminded me of an experience several years ago.

One morning, I was sitting on the couch and picked up a World Vision catalog. We were part of the child sponsorship program, and that month's newsletter advertised gifts to assist Majority World countries with community development. You could buy someone a goat for eighty dollars. I laughed as I thought of explaining the gift to Bonnie: "Sweetheart, happy Mother's Day! I know you have everything, so I bought you a goat in Zambia." Not sure how that would go over.

But as I thought about it more, I loved the idea of such giving (maybe Mother's Day would be one exception). Programs like Kiva and Hope International maximize capital investments in exponential ways. At the time, our church had been working with a village outside Lusaka, Zambia, for a couple of years, and the community was seeing fantastic improvement in their quality of life. Clean water, a medical center, a school, and life-sustaining agricultural practices were now present in this village. Our family could give a lot more than we were presently giving, I thought. Giving gifts through this type of program at holidays and birthdays would be a great way to shift our gift giving as well.

The mail came that afternoon, and in the stack was that month's edition of *Boating*. After we moved to Florida, my father-in-law had given me a subscription. As I walked back to the house, I looked at a deck boat and immediately pictured our family jetting up and down the Gulf Coast. Desire flooded my imagination, and suddenly our family needed a boat—for "family bonding," of course. I cared about our family spending time together, and this was the ticket. I took out my phone, quickly calculated the monthly costs, and even sketched out some possible ways to make it work with our budget. If we didn't eat every third day and borrowed gas money to fuel the boat, it wouldn't be much of a stretch.

A couple of minutes later, the irony revealed itself. The $80 goat and $27,000 deck boat were both looking at me with puzzling glances.

And here I was again, trying to add a completely different way of life on top of an already full and frenetic one, without any significant modifications. Mental preoccupation was the barrier, I thought, not a busy schedule. If only they could be so easily separated.

In time I discovered that if my body was constantly in a state of hurry, my mind would be as well. I couldn't just add "openness to the moment" as a new conceptual framework for life on top of all the others. Being open to the Spirit's presence would require a reorientation to life, including letting go of some things. An allowance for margin, a limiting of mental stimulation, a rhythm that incorporated rest, Sabbath, and spiritual disciplines of abstinence as well as engagement, and even the exercise of deepening my shallow breathing and relaxing my clenched jaw and shoulders: all these were part of the package when it came to living fully present to God.

I was enticed by the short visit to this new way of life, and the more I tried to embody it, the deeper the changes went. When I started my day with a sense of expectancy and a willingness to be inconvenienced, some incredible things happened. I've seen a few miracles and experienced a lot of encounters that felt like divine appointments.

You mean I'm just supposed to go up and *talk* to people?

Doing these four practices of healing presence—loving, listening, discerning, and responding—can be anxiety inducing at first. Just try it. Put down this book, go out into your neighborhood or a public place, and pray, "God, help me to see where you're at work. Help me to love, listen, discern, and respond." When you sense a small prompting to initiate a conversation with someone, rather than kill that prompting through introspection, respond to it. Now you'll see what I mean! Almost certainly you'll feel anxiety.

You can't look ahead to see where the road will take you. You may experience a significant breakthrough with someone. Then again, you may embarrass yourself or be rejected. At first, the potential for these unexpected breakthroughs doesn't register as a high enough reward to compensate for the accompanying fears and doubts.

Most of us are creatures of habit who like to know where the roads we walk are headed. We embrace the untold benefits of security, familiarity, predictability, and control. The more our experiences can embody these traits, the more comfortable we are. Cultivating the daily practices of loving, listening, discerning, and responding means cutting against the natural current of our preferences.

But the great news is that small breakthroughs become contagious and expand our faith. When the reality sets in—that God invites us to become conduits of God's presence and power to others—it places the background of life in an entirely different light. Other people are not merely the backdrop to our stories. Those we overlook possess intrinsic significance that would stop us in our tracks—far more than an accomplished violinist in a subway station—if we could only recognize it. The more attentive we are, the richer and fuller life becomes.

A conduit of the very presence and power of the living God

The ability to function as a conduit of God's presence and power to others it not something I can get my mind around. I don't even partially understand it. I just accept that there are some things we can know through experience that we're never able to rationally understand, let alone capture in words. What I know for sure is that the more receptive I am to God's presence in my daily life—the more willing I am to respond in faith to small promptings—the more I see God's intricate involvement in human affairs.

This single reality has brought about a significant paradigm shift for how I think of Christian ministry. Our ministry is not to be merely one of words. It is to be one of presence. Paul writes that "the kingdom of God is not a matter of talk but of power" (1 Corinthians 4:20). When we help people, we are not left to our own devices or wisdom. We need not limit God's Word to a handbook of cognitive and behavioral therapeutic interventions and assume that God himself is out of the picture.

I imagine a stage performance in which the play's creator and writer is on the stage during rehearsal. But the actors don't see the playwright. The actors absorb themselves in his script as they strive to get their roles right. All the while, they assume he has left the building. All the while, he is standing right there among them.

Intimacy fuels activity

In *The Screwtape Letters*, an imagined correspondence between a senior and junior demon, C. S. Lewis captures well the temptation for our work to replace intimacy with God as our main pursuit.

> Once you have made the World an end, and faith a means, you have almost won your man, and it makes very little difference what kind of worldly end he is pursuing. Provided that meetings, pamphlets, policies, movements, causes, and crusades matter more to him than prayers and sacraments and charity, he is ours—and the more "religious" (on those terms) the more securely ours. I could show you a pretty cageful down here.[3]

When we grasp the significance of the invitation to collaborate with God, life itself takes on a new dimension. Significance is no longer limited to achieving our goals. It's no longer just about the script. The world is charged with God's presence, and there is simply no limit, beyond our own internal barriers, to what God can accomplish. When people walk closely with God and embrace the vulnerability of a living faith, God does miracles. Achieving a personal goal is rewarding, but following a God-orchestrated detour leads to fullness of life.

We were meant to live in intimate fellowship with God. Many things today conspire against this. But when you begin to experience life in rhythm with God's Spirit, daily life is permeated with a fullness far beyond anything you could ever create yourself. When you pray, "God, in this moment, help me to be fully present to you and the people around me," your perspective changes. Even the best of our personal pursuits for achievement begin to feel a bit vacuous compared to life lived *coram Deo*: "before the face of God."

Those four words I was introduced to before the neighborhood prayer walk—*love, listen, discern,* and *respond*—help us begin to practice the healing presence of Christ. Let's start with love. We need to camp out here a bit, because if we can get this right, it will set everything that follows into right alignment.

4

A Love Differentiated

Two of the kids we've fostered over the years were four-year-old twins from a background of severe neglect. When they first came into our home, they wouldn't allow us to touch them. At night, the only bedtime routine they'd accept was us sitting in the doorframe until they fell asleep. Our stories of these girls are endless.

Slowly, however, they began to open up to small overtures of nurture. After about six or seven months, we could rock them to sleep, and they would even seek out comfort when they were hurt. It was an incredible transformation to see. But it was a painful one to walk through, because it wasn't as if they said, "No, thanks, I don't feel like a hug right now. Maybe next year." No. They'd hit you in the face and laugh. They'd plot against you. They'd pee on your couch if you upset them. (That one almost threw me over the edge.)

No matter. We couldn't give in and respond out of our instincts. They'd take our "love and logic" discipline attempts, light them on fire, and throw them back in our faces. Any trace of anger from us simply reinforced the disconnect they felt. Until there could be a real connection, there couldn't be healthy discipline. So as foster parents we had to try to absorb the pain as best we could.

Love does many things. One of the ways it heals is by absorbing unjust pain. Of course, loving a four-year-old foster child is easier than loving an adult who is responsible for our pain. In this chapter, we'll look at the ways of love, which is the first step in becoming a healing presence to the people around you.

A love not tethered to stimulus

If you've ever been to a wedding, you've probably heard 1 Corinthians 13 recited; it's the passage that includes "Love is patient; love is kind" (verse 4). During our premarital counseling sessions, Bonnie and I were taught to replace the word *love* with our names and then strive to ensure that we could recognize each other in the descriptions. "Wes is not easily angered. . . . Wes always protects, always trusts"; "Bonnie keeps no record of wrongs."

But the love chapter is seldom read to the end. After the opening descriptions of love, the chapter moves into some comments about childhood and adulthood that seem out of place at first glance. Verse 11 says, "When I was a child, I talked like a child, I thought like a child, I reasoned like a child. When I became a man, I put the ways of childhood behind me." What is the connection here to love?

The "ways of a child" are tethered to stimulus. Children are hopelessly reactive to their environment and circumstances. Our little nieces have a game I call Who Stole My Sippy Cup? Brooklyn, age three, steals her older sister's cup and runs away, laughing. She knows what's about to go down. Her older sister sees her, and a chase ensues. If Brighton catches her, she knocks her down and rescues her cup. On cue, Brooklyn cries, and Mommy tells Brighton she can't be so rough with her sister. Any guesses as to Brighton's defense? "She made me! She stole my sippy cup!" In other words, "I had no other choice because of what she did." There's a clear tethering between the stimulus (Brooklyn swiping the cup) and the response (Brighton knocking her over).

In 1 Corinthians 13, Paul is saying, "God's love isn't tethered to stimulus." *Love is patient*: even in unfavorable environments or circumstances, love remains patient. That's what love *is*.

A love not weakened by betrayal

When Jesus washes the disciples' feet before his crucifixion, he introduces a subtle but world-changing shift in our understanding of love. Even if you're familiar with this story, try to imagine this scene unfold as described in John 13:21-30:

> Jesus was troubled in spirit and testified, "Very truly I tell you, one of you is going to betray me."
>
> His disciples stared at one another, at a loss to know which of them he meant. One of them, the disciple whom Jesus loved, was reclining next to him. Simon Peter motioned to this disciple and said, "Ask him which one he means."
>
> Leaning back against Jesus, he asked him, "Lord, who is it?"
>
> Jesus answered, "It is the one to whom I will give this piece of bread when I have dipped it in the dish." Then, dipping the piece of bread, he gave it to Judas, the son of Simon Iscariot. As soon as Judas took the bread, Satan entered into him.
>
> So Jesus told him, "What you are about to do, do quickly." But no one at the meal understood why Jesus said this to him. Since Judas had charge of the money, some thought Jesus was telling him to buy what was needed for the festival, or to give something to the poor. As soon as Judas had taken the bread, he went out. And it was night.

Jesus never sees Judas after his betrayal. It's one of the scenes I wish were in the Bible. What would Jesus have said or done if he saw Judas after his betrayal? I think he would have said, "I forgive you! There's no need to remain bound to your sin." I think Jesus would have done everything in his power to reach Judas, look him in the eyes, and say, "Choose life! Don't go down this path. You're freed from it."

Here's why. What happens after this moment in the upper room is extraordinary. Right after Judas runs out, Jesus says, "A new command I give you: Love one another. As I have loved you, so you must love one another. By this everyone will know that you are my disciples, if you love one another" (John 13:34-35). Betrayal to the point of death is the context for these words, which are introduced in a way unlike any other teaching in the gospel. This is the only time in the gospel that Jesus says, "Here's a new command." The command to love isn't new. What's different is the phrase "as I have loved you."

You are to love people, not as they deserve or according to how you feel about them, but "as I have loved you."

Has anyone ever loved you in such a way? Have you ever been Judas: defenseless, ashamed, and ready to deal with the consequences? Has anyone met your betrayal with acceptance, responded to your anger with kindness, and even though you slandered their name, refused to speak or even believe anything about you but hope?

Any memory come to mind? Maybe not, and sometimes that's part of our struggle. We see Jesus washing the disciples' feet and asking them, "Do you understand what I've done?" They wouldn't at first. But then they'd remember: he didn't just wash my feet; he washed *Judas's* feet! He washed the feet of the man who would betray him to the point of death. Then they'd remember him standing up and saying, "Do as I've done to you. Love as I have loved you."

This love is stronger than death. This love expels fear, absorbs pain, and covers sin and shame. It is an import from heaven. We must allow ourselves to be drawn into this love before it can flow through us in our own times of hurt, betrayal, and suffering.

This is part of the struggle for Stephanie. She's a fierce protector of her boys and tries as hard as she can to love them. But trying to do the opposite of what you're familiar with can only take you so far. She knows nothing of love and isn't even comfortable speaking the word to her boys.

Imagine that Stephanie's boyfriend, Kevin, experiences a profound conversion and immerses himself in the Lord, learning to live into and out of the "unforced rhythms of [God's] grace" (Matthew 11:28-30, *The Message*). He learns to love and serve her, to put her needs and the needs of their boys above his own. He sees the fear beneath her angry outbursts and pulls her in close when she pushes him away. He meets her cursing with blessing. Over time, her defenses will soften. His kindness will disarm her criticisms. His nonanxious presence and unwillingness to bend into her or abandon her will force her to become present to the deeper issues in her heart. His belief in her will undercut deep fears and insecurity. Unreciprocated animosity is a vexing challenge. No Judas can stand for long before such love and remain unchanged. It's why the apostle Paul said that such love does not fail.

Aesop wrote, "Kindness is more effective than severity." Proverbs 25 recommends the practice of giving one's enemies food when they are hungry and water when they are thirsty—to "heap burning coals" (verse 22) on their heads will awaken their conscience. Wisdom supports the exchange of blessing for cursing as the recipe for breaking cycles of retribution. But it is Jesus alone who brings to us a love that is stronger than death and the power to experience it.

A love that sees clearly

When Robin was twenty-one years old, she rarely had contact with her mother or grandparents. She was living by herself, selling jewelry, and dating a DJ because, in her words, "he could get me free drinks." She would drink heavily most nights, wake up the next day, and do it all again. For some reason, one night she was hit with an overwhelming feeling of being lost. She drove to the Catholic church her grandparents took her to as a child. "I sat in the parking lot in the middle of the night quietly weeping," Robin reflects now. "I went there to talk with God, whoever he was . . . I was so confused, so destructive, but I wanted to do life better."

Nothing earth-shattering happened that night, but a couple of weeks later, she met her boyfriend's mother, which became the turning point in her life. "Jon and I didn't have a very healthy relationship." Robin laughs as she says it. "But his mom wanted to meet me." Robin had never met anyone like her. She was a Spirit-filled schoolteacher who hugged Robin the first time she met her. "She took a strange interest in me," Robin recounts. "She listened to me, encouraged me, and accepted me. Margaret was the first person in my life to ever make me feel like I mattered, without any expectations or strings attached. It was the unconditional, healing love of God."

Robin was over at Margaret's house one evening and was feeling sick, and she asked if she could pray for her. Margaret placed her hands on Robin, prayed for her healing, and began to share the gospel message with her. Fully receptive, Robin remembers thinking, "I want whatever she has. She was the most loving, joyful, and peaceful person I had ever met."

Robin's boyfriend, the woman's son, wasn't too happy about this. A lot changed in Robin's life, and quickly. She says now, "I kept telling him, 'We've got to do this Jesus thing together.'" He wasn't interested, and pretty soon they broke up. But his mother continued to disciple Robin and help her develop a passion for God's Word and prayer. She never told Robin to stop certain behaviors, but she told her, "The closer you get to Jesus, the more you'll see your desires start to change."

One of the themes of their meetings was a reframing of Robin's story with an understanding of God's love and redemption. Margaret helped Robin to see her past in a very different light than she had before, and to walk through a forgiveness process with her family. "None of it will be wasted," she said to Robin constantly. "You'll see. Your story isn't one of rejection. It's one of redemption. God is going to use you to help a lot of people."

Robin moved to Florida about six months after she met this woman. But she says that meeting Margaret was when her life changed: "She introduced me to Jesus and was the first person to show me love."

Distinguish the source and object of love

When you look closely at people who embody life-giving love at places of death, you find an unexpected power source. Like a besieged city with a hidden and inexhaustible spring flowing through its center, the source and object of their love are differentiated; they are not the same.

Such people, who progress well in Jesus' school of love, are able to love in seemingly transcendent ways because they are deeply rooted in God's transcendent love. It's not a mere intellectual assent to a doctrine. It's a deeply spiritual reality, as real as anything they confront that may challenge it. They are *in* love, as much as they are "in" any given circumstance, because they are *in* Christ. This phrase—"in Christ"—occurs ninety-two times in the New Testament. What does that mean?

When we live in the knowledge that we are in Christ, people and circumstances are not ultimately sovereign over our lives. God is sovereign. He is our Redeemer. God is able to affirm our identity, meet our needs, drive out our fears, and wash us of the effects of sin. As the apostle Paul writes, we are "being rooted and established in [God's] love" (Ephesians 3:17). When we are in Christ, we are able to cast our burdens on the Lord, and he keeps us in peace as we keep our eyes on him. The effect of our grounding in God's love is that we don't look to others to repay every debt they owe us. We forgive debts, just as we are forgiven. As we forgive, we bring the recipients face-to-face with unmerited grace.

You can think of this distinction between the source and object of our love in the light of philanthropy. A philanthropist draws a great deal of money from one source and chooses to give it freely to another source. The source and the recipient are clearly distinguished. In Jesus' new commandment, he does the same with the source and recipients of our love. We are to love people, not as they deserve or according to how we feel about them, but as Jesus has loved us. God is the source; people are the recipients.

The power to love like this, especially when you've been deeply wounded, is a gift from God. As we allow God's love to excavate our soul and reshape our perspective, our own capacity to love in ways and places that seem impossible grows exponentially. We no longer look to people to set everything right, repay outstanding debts, and fill every void. We're no longer tethered to stimulus. Jesus' love, which is patient, kind, slow to anger, and keeps no record of wrongs, is what grounds and roots our very identity. It washes us of fear and covers sin and shame. It's the most beautiful and powerful gift anyone has ever received. God's love absorbs pain.

Twenty-one days to love

How do you love a person who has hurt you? Where does the pain go? Several years ago, I read 1 Corinthians 13 and felt myself slipping back into old patterns that were not so loving. I took the next twenty-one days and read this chapter each morning. Each morning I prayed, "God, help me to receive and extend your love today, no matter what happens." At the end of each day, I took out 1 Corinthians 13 and prayed it again, first in self-examination: "God, where did your love manifest today through my actions and speech? Where did it not?" Then, I simply meditated on it. Reading 1 Corinthians 13 each day for twenty-one days was like praying a three-week-long, soaking prayer: "God, empower me to love as you love, because right now it's not happening."

Not surprisingly, during that period, God gave me ample opportunities for growth. More than a good cognitive exercise, this twenty-one-day experiment was a spiritual practice leading me toward love. Through it, God excavated areas of unforgiveness, pulled up some bitter root judgments (see Hebrews 12:15), and slowly began to give power to find redemption in suffering.

God can bear our pain. He can heal our hearts. He can meet our needs according to his riches in glory. God will bring to fullness the work he's started. As these truths started to sink in, my tethering to stimulus was slowly breaking. With it, my capacity to love sacrificially grew.

Compassion is an expression of God's sacrificial love, and it's the greatest gift in the world. We can learn to love when it's not reciprocated. The source and object of our love are not the same. And when this untethering happens in us, our capacity for compassion expands to a whole new level.

5

The Doorway to Healing

U h-huh, yeah, that's awesome, bud."
My eyes were glancing back and forth between my son Max and my phone. He was showing me the difference between two new Lego cars he had built. I was reading a news story. He didn't call attention to my lack of attention; he just walked away.

As he did, that tinge of conviction set in, so I set my phone down and chased him into the kitchen, scooping him up. "Sorry! Let me see it again."

In the fourfold gift of healing presence—love, listen, discern, and respond—undistracted and nonjudgmental listening is often the front door. In ways words never could, the gift of listening conveys worth. "You're worth listening to," the one listening says to the other person. "Your voice needs to be heard." In this chapter we'll examine the power of listening in the work of healing presence.

Listening without judgment

When we first met the parents of the twins we fostered, it was an awkward scene. They were embarrassed and assumed our judgment and contempt of them. So naturally they were guarded and defensive. No one wants to spend time with, let alone receive any help from, people who judge them. "You can keep your condescending charity. We're good here."

Frankly, the relationship was set up for failure. We had their kids in our home because the state had judged them to be unfit parents at the moment. Addiction had ravaged their home, and the level of neglect was severe enough to warrant the children's removal.

Our first meeting was at a park. We brought pizza and had a two-hour play date. The girls were thrilled to see them. Their father and I pushed the girls on the swings and talked. We spoke about his daughters' unique traits and made-up words. The girls spoke a language only they understood, and we laughed as we tried to repeat some of their phrases.

It was a fairly pleasant evening without any serious conversations. Toward the end of the evening, the girls' father began to rail against the investigator, who he said had lied in his report. "There were no drugs in the house," he said. Bonnie and I just listened and didn't say much. As we said goodbye, we reinforced our role as a support for their family, including them personally, our commitment to their girls during this time, and our hope for their reunification.

We didn't want to pretend things were different than they were. Nor did we want to stand in the place of judgment. These parents didn't need false platitudes disconnected from reality. They had created a serious mess, and to minimize the effects of their choices would be unjust. Truth was important. But any judgment or contempt would also be ineffective. They expected it and were prepared to resist it. They expected rejection rather than acceptance, lectures rather than listening.

So first, we would need to take a seat next to them, see the view, and hear their voices. Only then, from a place of trust and acceptance, could we slowly begin to interject hope toward new life. No trust, no influence. Again, the posture of compassion begins with proximity, solidarity, and emotional connectedness.

Listening fully and without judgment has a way of relaxing people's defense mechanisms and setting the stage for a healing journey. They begin to sense that this is a safe place in which to be somewhat real. Not all at once, for sure. It happens layers at a time, like the waves of the ocean gently rolling onto the seashore.

Imagine this father's predicament with me. When he meets me, he is likely contemplating two choices: being honest, vulnerable, and willing to work toward restoration or, conversely, giving way to self-protection, fear, and pride. My presence isn't inconsequential as he chooses his path forward. How do I create an environment as conducive to life and redemption as possible?

He is at a delicate and scary place in life, and the vulnerability required for him to reject pretense and be somewhat real requires a huge amount of humility and courage. My undistracted and non-judgmental listening are absolutely critical as a starting point. At the first sign of rejection, judgment, or indifference, his fears will be confirmed, and my opportunity to be a part of his healing journey will vanish.

Think about the road ahead for him. His entire ecosystem resists any movement toward healing. Layers of resentment and shame will need to be uncovered. Lies that distort his self-image will need to be replaced with truth. Hopefully, he'll begin to bring truths hidden in darkness into the light and align his will with goodness and truth. Deuteronomy 30:19 reminds us of the choice below every choice: "I have set before you life and death, blessings and curses. Now choose life, so that you and your children may live." For his sake and the sake of his family, this father will need to learn to calibrate his "yeses and nos" in line with what God names "life and death." Eventually.

At the point we meet, confusion and chaos reign, and stabilization is the modest goal. Choosing life in this moment is simply not giving in to death and despair. My temptation is to try and rush him along the behavioral pathways to healing and restoration. I see both the wreckage and the solution. It's easy to see from my vantage point. Like a horror movie where you think, "Why would you walk through that door?" I want to ask him, "Don't you see what's on the other side of that choice? Don't do it!" But that would be a mistake.

Undistracted and nonjudgmental listening doesn't necessitate a whitewashing of truth. It builds and preserves the relational bridge required for truth to cross. When we try to stand up in an ash heap—especially one we created—and begin the slow, uncertain, and painful stagger toward redemption, there's nothing like the gift of those who listen. There's nothing like having others see us for who we are and stick by our side with a peaceful, differentiated, and steadying presence. They don't give up when we're at our worst and walk away shaking their head in contempt. They don't lose patience or shove our face in our shame. But neither do they affirm our bad judgment or pat us on the back as we plunge head-long over a cliff. Undistracted, nonjudgmental listening is a crucial component of the gift of healing presence.

Listening toward recovery

When I first met Robin, the woman whose boyfriend's mother had led her to Christ, she was a talented and successful director of a media company. She worked with clients like author and speaker John Maxwell, and she was coordinating some media projects for our church and a nonprofit we were running. Robin would show up to meetings absolutely full of life. She lights up every room she enters.

For the first two years I knew Robin, she kept her tumultuous past in the dark. I never would have guessed that she was dropped off at church because her driver's license had been revoked after her third DUI. Even though she was a member of our church, all our conversations were related to joint projects and in the context of larger groups.

I wish I had known what she was going through.

One night, I got a call on my cell phone from a woman who said, "I'm with Robin Bright, and you might want to come over to her house right now." The woman explained that Robin's entire family was there. Robin's alcohol addiction had long ravaged the family, and they had decided that it was finally time for her to get treatment.

When I first walked in the house, it was hard to mask my shock. Dozens of empty liquor bottles were strewn all over the house, and Robin was sitting in the middle of the living room floor surrounded by her sister, daughters, and a close family friend. You could feel the daughters' own internal conflict as they made statements like,

"Well, Mom, you know what you have to do." It was clear that they had all been here many times before.

Her daughters were not able to offer much in the way of comfort. Their lives had been significantly shaped by their mother's addiction. Memories of homelessness, divorce, and a lost childhood were too thick to see through to hope. But they were there with her. They hadn't abandoned her.

It was Robin's sister, Shelby whose presence made the difference in this moment. I had been in these places plenty of times before, and it was usually easy to see the "helper" vacillate between enabling and condemning. In these situations, you expected to hear the courtroom judgment: "You've made a big enough mess, so that's it. We're taking over from here." But this friend had been with her from the beginning; she knew the good, the bad, the ugly. Nothing was hidden.

Picture this: Robin and her sister Shelby were sitting side by side on the floor. Robin's head drooped listlessly on Shelby's shoulder. Shelby rubbed Robin's head and listened to a long, painful, contradictory, rambling, and slurred account of Robin's struggles. She was a victim. She was hopeless. Nothing was wrong. Nothing could be salvaged. Everyone hated her. No one understood her. She contaminated everything. It would be better if she weren't alive. She just needed to be left alone.

I expected Shelby to interrupt and correct her, but she didn't. She just kept rubbing Robin's head. When Robin finally ran out of gas, Shelby put her arms around her and simply said, "You're going to get through this. You will get better. This isn't your fate. There's one choice we need to make today. What do you think?"

The conversation then went to the pros and cons of recovery programs. After another long, meandering explanation of why it wasn't necessary, and why those programs don't work, and the impact that being in such a program would have on her job, Robin paused. Shelby affirmed the few statements Robin had made about needing help and said, "Can we make a call right now and see what you think?"

I had recommended a detox and treatment center, and the question on the table was whether Robin should wait a week to tie up some important business or try to get help immediately, regardless of the consequences. Her daughters were emotionally distant but verbally adamant: "You need to go somewhere right now and deal with this once and for all. You've only cared about consequences and never tried to get to the root of the problem."

Shelby was patient and kind. She believed and hoped. The towering heap of broken promises and past failures had been leveled in her mind, and she was able to sit next to Robin, in her personal ground zero, with a heart to bless.

By this point, it was pretty late in the evening. Shelby stayed with Robin, and we agreed to meet the next morning and drive to the treatment center. Today, Robin is in long-term recovery and active in the recovery community. She has become an advocate for effective intervention strategies and lowering the cultural stigma of addiction. She's not anonymous. In her words, "I'm an open book. If my story can help someone, I don't want to keep it secret. I'm done hiding."

As her former boyfriend's mom had once called it, Robin's story is one of catalytic redemption. Dozens and probably hundreds of people now point to Robin's work as directly instrumental in their own recovery. Several say, "She literally saved my life." You'll meet a couple of these people and hear their stories in the pages ahead.

You should hear Robin talk about Shelby. It's not her advice you'll hear about; it's her presence. Shelby was there in the mess, repeatedly, and stayed by Robin's side with a peaceful, differentiated, and steadying presence always oriented toward life.

Lessons from a teenage daughter

Right now, my teenage daughter, Alex, is the one teaching me the importance of connection for influence. The main critique teens level against their parents is that they don't understand them. In our home, it's absolutely true. I don't understand. Intense and fluctuating emotions seem to appear and then disappear, without any clear correlation to what's going on in the moment. Sometimes

Alex walks out of a room and I ask Bonnie, "What just happened?" I get dizzy trying to keep up.

What's been alarming for me at times is the feeling of disconnection. This is more than the normal pull toward independence; it's an increasing relational disconnect between us. Frankly, the blame is on me. Sometimes it's a matter of preoccupation and not valuing enough the topic of conversation, which is often the daily relational drama at school. I tend to offer quick, matter-of-fact solutions and try to deescalate the severity of the situation and the intensity of the emotion. I try not to, but it's so tempting to say, "Alex, if you think that's a big deal, you're in for quite a shock. When I was your age . . ." Those are such fun conversations.

Other times, I find myself cutting Alex off or not listening to everything she says. Subtle judgments, dismissive corrections, and a heavy dose of sarcasm is a cocktail of rejection, and not just to teenage girls. It's certainly never intentional, but I often manage to focus on the topic at hand rather than on my daughter's heart. I may hear what she says and yet fail to listen to her voice. The distinction is between attending to the words themselves, and my reaction to them, and attending to her heart *beneath* the words. If my mind is busy formulating my response while she's speaking, my mind is not focused on her heart. Luke 6:45 reminds us of the connection between heart and words: out of the overflow of the heart, the mouth speaks. The focus of the Scripture is on speech, but on the listening side of things, we can follow the cord down to the heart as well and see the importance of tending well to the source.

This disconnect with Alex—my struggle to listen well to her, and her pulling away—is a relatively new phenomenon in our family. I'm not a fan of all the changes of adolescence, and I simply haven't adjusted well. At times it looks as if we are headed toward that scene in the movie *Brave* where the mother and her teenage daughter both scream at the same time, "Why won't you just *listen*?"

So the other day I took her out for ice cream. After a long mea culpa, I said, "Sweetheart, we love you and we all want the same thing for you. It may not feel this way, but we're all headed in the same direction . . . and we'll get there. We want you to be a thriving, healthy adult, and we're not going to try and hold you in a childlike posture. Does it feel like we're trying to hold you back?"

"No, but it doesn't feel like you trust me," she said.

"How could we communicate trust better?" I asked her.

"Well, let me ride my bike outside the neighborhood, and don't check my phone like I'm some sort of compulsive liar," she began. "Let me spend the night at a friend's house without first interrogating their parents and checking the batteries in their smoke alarms. And if it's PG-13, let me watch it; I'm fourteen!"

Alex had clearly thought about this a few times before this conversation.

"Okay, we can talk through those," I said with a smile. "That's quite a list."

"Oh, there's more." She smiled back.

Alex shared some recent frustrations, and we talked about ways to create space for more independence and time away without disconnecting from our family. At some point, I said, "In the big picture, these three years until you graduate are like a short walk across a bridge. I hope we can be patient with each other and not lose our connection."

A couple of tears ran down my cheek as I said those last words. This surprised her, because I'm known to be emotionally constipated. There was a long pause, but she didn't bail me out. She didn't know what to say.

"For your mom and me, if we can be vulnerable, this whole 'launching' thing is conflicting," I continued. "In our heads, we want you to gain independence and thrive; but in our hearts, we love being your parents and don't want to lose you. See our conflict? We like having you around here! We know our job isn't to raise up a child, but the young woman I'm looking at now and the baby I first put in the car seat for the scariest drive in my life aren't as far apart as you imagine."

Again, a few more tears. It was time to wrap it up. "So," I said, and grabbed her hands, "here's my question: When we err and trip over each other during this short transition, can we lean in together and not allow our relationship to fray?"

This good and much-needed conversation released a lot of frustration and reset the equilibrium between us. Without a strong, relational connection, our ability to influence will be greatly diminished. In some relationships, we can possibly guilt, shame, manipulate, or coerce behaviors. But that's not the kind of influence we want. Listening well, in ways that communicate acceptance and fully attend to the heart, open the pathways for a healing presence.

6

Three Ways to Usher in New Life

Differentiated love and full attentiveness are essential to culti-vating a healing presence with others. In Genesis 16, God himself offers these very things to a woman on the verge of losing her identity. She was the maidservant to Abram and Sarai. When it appeared to Abram that God's promise of children in his old age needed a little boost, Abram used her to make it happen. The woman became a commodity for the family, significant only to the degree of her usefulness. When she was no longer useful, she was discarded. Abram and Sarai's conversation about her is instructive:

> Then Sarai said to Abram, "You are responsible for the wrong I am suffering. I put my slave in your arms, and now that she knows she is pregnant, she despises me. May the Lord judge between you and me."

> "Your slave is in your hands," Abram said. "Do with her what-ever you think best." (Genesis 16:5-6)

What's missing in the entire conversation is her name. She's a commodity, not a person. She's "my slave," "your slave," "she," and "her," but never Hagar. Outside of the narrator's voice, the first time someone actually speaks her name in the story occurs in verse 8, when the angel finds her in the wilderness, where she has fled after being mistreated. The first word out of the angel's mouth is "Hagar."

The angel helps Hagar regain her bearings and promises to provide for her. The story ends with Hagar doing something no one else does in the entire Bible: she names God! "She gave this name to the Lord who spoke to her: 'You are the God who sees me,' for she said, 'I have now seen the One who sees me'" (Genesis 16:13).

What the angel does for Hagar we must do for others at their place of suffering. When it comes time to speak life, two initial needs are countering the voice of slander and accusation and removing any cloak of shame. Dante's depiction of Satan in *Inferno* is instructive here: he's trapped in a block of ice. He cannot change; he cannot become anything other than who and what he is. The inability to change is the source of despair.

Loving and listening lead to the last two practices of healing presence: discerning and responding. Discernment and response to other people's pain and suffering mean that we are speaking life into existence. In this chapter, we'll look first at slander and shame in order to remember how easy it is to speak death instead of life. Then we'll investigate three ways of discerning and responding to those in our community: the Barnabas way, the Emmaus way, and the prophetic way.

Unfreezing fatalism

Slander is etymologically tied to the word *devil*. To slander another is to give our voice to the devil—the accuser—and speak untruth, which includes anything that's not oriented toward life.

The easy test for truth would appear to be, did it happen? In the case of Robin, the truth was she was an addict who had brought considerable harm on others. Many related and discouraging truths could coalesce and build momentum all the way to hell. Her daughters and friend could have given their voices to name truth and consequences in a way that cut through her. This is the meaning of *diabolic*: to cut through.

But the question of truth must be viewed in light of God's character as well as circumstance. I can speak truth that is circumstantially accurate, but if my speech is not reflective of God's character, it actually offers a warped view of truth. Like goodness and beauty, truth is inseparable from God's character. God names good and evil, life and death. Truth demarcates the distinctions. If we connect truth and God's character, we can never justify sidestepping love in the pursuit of truth. We must recognize that when we feel obligated to veer off the path of love, we veer from God. God *is* love. God *is* life, and everything of God flows toward life like water flows downstream.

Imagine if Robin's sister Shelby had said to her, "You've failed every attempt at recovery, and there's no reason to think this time will be any different." It's an accurate statement, in one sense: it reflects circumstances. It's not untrue. Her words, however, would "cut through" Robin and blur an essential aspect of God's character. God traffics in life in every proverbial graveyard on this planet. Instead of this "truthful" statement, which would cut through Robin and speak death instead of life, Shelby's approach was something like, "Yeah, we've been here before. But today is a new day, and God is giving you everything you need to step fully into life and walk this healing journey toward redemption, in which nothing needs to be wasted." By itself, the first statement would be slanderous because it would cut through life and, in so doing, misrepresent truth.

Slander should never be mistaken for a tool to protect truth or awaken another to life. Slander has no place on the lips of followers of Jesus, people who wear empty crosses around their necks to remind them of the single event that divided human history and completely changed our view and experience of life and death. God specializes in bringing life from death. It's the center of our faith. With Jesus, we stand over death, wherever we find it, and never lose sight of the fact that the very power that raised Christ from the dead is available to us. Life from death is a core truth for followers of Jesus. Slanderous speech—fatalistic words that freeze people in their sin and suffering—is always untrue, regardless of how accurate it may seem to be circumstantially.

Uncloaking shame
We were in Busch Gardens once and overheard a father scream at his son, "You want me to rip your bloody head off?! Is that

what you want?" Now, he said it in a British accent, so it sounded more sophisticated and polite, somehow, to our ears. The boy was crying, "No, Daddy." Evidently, the son had stolen something from the store. The father continued, "Is this the kind of person you are? Do you want to be known as a liar and thief? Shame on you!" The father then walked away as his boy cried hysterically.

Clearly, the father was trying to motivate his son to make better choices. His intentions were probably noble. The subtext of his comments was, "This *isn't* who you are. This decision runs counter to who you are." But that's not what his son heard.

Shame is a word that almost defies definition. Its root word means "to cover." In Scripture, you'll often find the verb "to cover," before the nominal form "shame." Psalm 34:5 says, "Those who look to him are radiant; their faces are never covered with shame." Shame is a covering. In the beginning, God created Adam and Eve, and they were naked and felt no shame. It's not a commentary on clothing. It's the recognition that nothing is hidden. Everything is in the open. But after Adam and Eve eat the fruit from the tree of the knowledge of good and evil, they do two things as God approaches: they cover themselves, and they hide (Genesis 3:7-8). This is one of the most tragic passages in the Bible: God draws close to people and they run, out of fear and shame.

Shame is different from guilt. We feel guilt for something we've done. We feel shame for who we are. "I did, therefore I am." After we watched the father berate his son, the child buried his face in his hands. When his mother tried to console him, he wouldn't look up at her. It was as if his father draped a blanket of shame over his head and said, "See how this feels." Shame seeps deep into our skin. We're porous to such words, and it's difficult to distinguish the shaming from one's true self.

Shame is one of Satan's deadliest weapons, because it paralyzes you. It insulates you from God's grace. You may hear and even cognitively believe in God's grace, but it's not for you. You're *dis*-graced, a synonym for shame. You're immune to God's attempts to redeem and heal your past. You're sealed off from the truth of

God's Word that would usher you into abundant life, and you are shielded from God's blessing and calling on your life.

There's a story in John 8 in which a woman is caught in the act of adultery. She's dragged into the temple courtyard to be stoned to death. Jesus is teaching nearby, and the religious leaders see it as an opportunity to trap him. They expect he'll want to be soft on her, which means he'll need to contradict the law. Either way, they'll win. They stand her in front of him and say, "According to the law, she should be stoned for her sins. What do you say?" Jesus replies with absolute brilliance, "Go ahead. But the one of you without sin go first" (John 8:7, my paraphrase). One by one, they drop their stones and walk away. The woman is left facing the only one who could condemn her, and he chooses not to. "Go now and leave your life of sin," he says (verse 11).

It's a good story when you read it from the vantage point of an onlooker. It's something altogether different when you read it from the perspective of the woman. All your possible accusers encircle you, and everything you've ever done is hurled back in your face. Then, suddenly, God himself walks up, and shame diminishes you even further. Yet without saying a word, God steps through all your accusers, grabs your shoulders, and embraces you. He frees you from the entanglement of sin to step fully into new life.

God's mercy leads us to repentance. You have your accusers. But they do not speak for God, and God is not with them, no matter how they use his name or bend his teachings. Yes, God will convict us when we veer from his best and highest for our lives. We need to respond to conviction with repentance. But with God, it's always a turn to life and its redemption.

If we are to be conduits of the presence and power of the living God, our words must be purged of all slander and shame. Even when we're peering into a pit of death, we must always speak and believe for life. No matter how deep the despair or far along someone is on the path to death, there is never a legitimate cause for fatalism. God's best work is often on the ash heap.

Our responses to people can always be oriented towards life. Let's look at three ways we can speak life into existence. The

Barnabas way means offering a personal blessing spoken in faith. The Emmaus way is a threefold movement that facilitates self-discovery and life change. The prophetic way offers specific, timely, and constructive words directly inspired by the Holy Spirit. As you become a conduit of God's healing presence to others, you will find which of these three ways, or combination thereof, flows most naturally out of your spirit and personality and which way fits best with each relationship.

The Barnabas way

Barnabas was a Greek Jew who was born on the wrong side of the tracks. His name was Joseph, and after responding in faith to the gospel message, he immediately sold land and laid the proceeds at the disciples' feet; this is the first recorded gift in the book of Acts. No strings were attached: it was an act of joyous, liberating generosity. Joseph's name was changed to Barnabas, which means "son of encouragement."

As the story progresses, it becomes clear that Barnabas's life mission isn't really about Barnabas. When Paul arrives in Jerusalem, Barnabas is the only person willing to give him a chance. He advocates for Paul and mentors him. In the early days of their mission work together, "Barnabas and Paul" experience tremendous breakthroughs in the face of overwhelming adversity. As the work expands, "Paul and Barnabas" (note that the order of their names is reversed) move into uncharted territory far beyond the Jewish areas in Asia Minor. Later, Paul is accepted as the apostle to the Gentiles and eventually pens half the books in the New Testament. Meanwhile, Barnabas fades into the background. There's not a book in the New Testament with Barnabas's name on it, but his imprint is all over it.

Consider for a moment this scene from Acts 15:36-40:

> Some time later Paul said to Barnabas, "Let us go back and visit the believers in all the towns where we preached the word of the Lord and see how they are doing." Barnabas wanted to take John, also called Mark, with them, but Paul did not think it wise to take him, because he had deserted them in Pamphylia and had not continued with them in the work. They had such a sharp

disagreement that they parted company. Barnabas took Mark and sailed for Cyprus, but Paul chose Silas and left, commended by the believers to the grace of the Lord.

Think about this conflict between Barnabas and Paul. Imagine the underlying values in tension. It's easy to imagine Paul's objection to Barnabas's insistence on including Mark. Here's how I imagine the conversation:

Paul: *Barnabas, you know as well as I do that the best predictor of future behavior is past behavior. And what does Mark's past behavior tell us to expect? He's a deserter. The man caves when the pressure grows. We can't risk that this time.*

Barnabas: *Don't define him by a low moment. There's a lot more God has for Mark than even he knows, and we can't give up on him. I promise you: he'll rise to the occasion. Grace, as you preach it so eloquently, is a powerful force.*

Paul: *But he doesn't have it in him. I'm a good judge of character, and he just doesn't have it.*

Barnabas: *That's funny. I distinctly remember hearing the exact same things said about you.*

The disagreement creates such a row between them that they split up and head in different directions. Time proves, however, that Barnabas was correct about John Mark, just as he was about Paul. Fast forward the story several years, and you'll find Paul requesting Mark's presence: "Get Mark and bring him with you," Paul writes, "because he is helpful to me in my ministry" (2 Timothy 4:11).

Mark changed, and Barnabas's belief had something to do with it. It's quite possible that during his time with Barnabas, Mark began to write what will become the first gospel of the New Testament.

Barnabas is able to discern and speak life where it is latent but not fully realized. I've had mentors do something similar over the years. They have seen potential in me that I didn't see, and they have spoken with the intent of blessing and calling forward my true self. They always spoke carefully rather than definitively. They never said, "This is the word of the Lord for you!" Instead, they said things like, "I see this in you, and I wonder if this is a part of you that you need to cultivate and pay more attention to."

For "Barnabas speech" to have significant impact, it needs to be spoken within a relational context and be supported with action. Barnabas is close to Paul and Mark. He is in the arena with them. He also backs up his words with a willingness to help bring them to life. It's one thing to say, "I know you don't think it's possible, and there's a lot that conspires against it, but I think you should really consider _____." It's another thing altogether to follow that up with, "And if you sense it's right, I'm ready to walk with you toward it."

Barnabas changes the world because, in his eyes, the world is bigger than Barnabas. He doesn't set out for greatness; he simply calls out greatness in others and leverages whatever he can to bring it to life.

His funeral must have been inspiring. "Sons of encouragement," over time, birth many sons, daughters, and grandchildren, who look back to those early blessings and investments as turning points. Mark probably said, "There wouldn't be a gospel of Mark without Barnabas." Paul perhaps would have said something similar. Untold others likely added their own versions of big and little encounters with a man who found ways to speak life into existence.

Are you a son or daughter of encouragement? When you respond to people in your neighborhood and community, do you, like Barnabas, speak into being their God-given potential? Do you not only speak the words but also offer to walk with them into their calling? Who do you know who could benefit from the Barnabas way?

The Emmaus way

The Emmaus road story in Luke provides another compelling model for responding to people. The experience along the Emmaus road is an extraordinary encounter that leads to a complete change of direction. The way that Jesus leads these disciples to a place of self-discovery establishes a pattern for us to follow.

In Luke 24:13-35, just after Jesus' resurrection, Jesus meets up with two disciples as they, bewildered and traumatized, flee Jerusalem. "What are you discussing together?" he asks them. Jesus draws out their shattered vision and disillusionment. "We had hoped he was the one who was going to redeem Israel," they tell him sadly.

Jesus then connects the dots from the past to present to reframe their vision. The three of them arrive at a town as the sun is about to set, and the two disciples extend hospitality to Jesus, saying, "Stay with us, for it is nearly evening." Then, at the table, after Jesus takes bread, gives thanks, breaks the bread, and gives it to them, their eyes suddenly open and they recognize Jesus. Once they see and understand, he departs. They do a one-eighty and return to Jerusalem to join the disciples in their work of extending Jesus' ministry.

Let's look more closely at the three movements of the Emmaus way. First, Jesus draws the disciples toward understanding through *questions* ("What do you see?"). Second, he uses *narrative* to help reframe their perspective ("What's the real story here?"). Finally, at the table, he extends the gift of *hospitality*, and their eyes are suddenly opened ("Let's eat together."). In each, Jesus guides the process but doesn't force the outcome. The Emmaus way model of responding to people—asking them questions to draw them out, offering them a narrative to reframe, and sharing hospitality— offers a powerful way of facilitated personal discovery for others.

When Jesus first encounters these two disciples, there is a clear disconnect between their hearts, which are in Jerusalem, and their bodies, which are headed full steam out of town. They have some level of knowledge of Jesus' resurrection, but they're still fleeing the scene. Their hopes may not have completely vanished, but neither are they remotely realized. Jesus could easily clear things up the moment he approaches. Why doesn't he? These disciples have been tossed about on an emotional roller coaster, and the gravity of the events in question rules out short explanations and quick fixes. First, Jesus needs to draw close and draw out. With a loving, differentiated presence and full attentiveness, he gives them the space to name the pieces of their incoherent narrative. "We thought . . ." they stumble. "We hoped . . ."

I sometimes tell Bonnie, "I need to talk through something to see what I really think about it." I can't do it all in my head. This is especially true when an event triggers a deeper reaction and I find myself in a quagmire of desire, fears, beliefs, and perspectives pulling in different directions. I'll verbally walk down a path for a while, only to realize it's the wrong path. As I hear myself name a possible perspective, I'll think, "No, this isn't right; this is fear talking." Bonnie's attentive listening and companionship is such a gift. She helps my head and heart stay connected, and she helps me identify the root issues. Often in these moments I find that an immediate response to the trigger would be the wrong response. Once I can set aside my disordered fears and identify my misplaced desires, there will be an epiphany.

Once these disciples have given voice to their fragmented perspective, Jesus reframes the events within a coherent and alternative narrative. "These events" (namely, Jesus' crucifixion), which are the source of their disillusionment, are not only essential to God's work; these events serve as the decisive turning point in history. Jesus asks, "Did not the Messiah have to suffer these things and then enter his glory?" (Luke 24:26). In the next verse, "beginning with Moses and all the Prophets," Jesus explains "what was said in all the Scriptures concerning himself." As the disciples take on this new perspective, they evidently see the events more clearly, but they do not recognize Jesus yet.

In Luke's writings, hospitality often opens the door to God's presence, and the disciples' invitation to Jesus to "stay" with them will be forever decisive in this regard. In the pattern established in the miraculous feeding of the multitude (Luke 9:16) and the Last Supper (Luke 22:19), here Jesus takes the bread, gives thanks (*eucharist*), breaks the bread, and gives it to them. Communion with Christ opens their eyes to his true identity. Suddenly, their downcast spirits are invigorated, their disillusionment coalesces into coherence, and they choose to return to Jerusalem.

The Emmaus way begins with a drawing close and a drawing out: side by side, walking together, one asks questions with full attentiveness to the other person's voice. Here, the focus is fully on the other: "What do you see?" The second movement shifts the perspective from the person, to other competing narratives: "What's the real story here?" When you offer an alternative and fully coherent perspective of the same events, you can piece together brokenness and disillusionment. The third movement of hospitality—"Let's eat together"—is where the real transformation takes place. This only happens if there is receptivity to Jesus. Here the focus shifts again, this time from the competing narratives to Jesus himself. An encounter with the living God is what ultimately brings the kind of change we see in this story, in which there is literally a 180-degree change of direction.

The prophetic way

Another way to be a conduit of God's presence and power is by voicing Spirit-inspired words of life. God chooses to speak through people, sometimes even with pinpoint precision. The apostle Paul instructs us, "Do not treat prophesies with contempt but test them all" (1 Thessalonians 5:20-21).

My first experience with Spirit-inspired words occurred when a man in our church, George, scheduled a meeting with me. We had never met before, and after introductions and some small talk, he said, "First, I feel like I need to tell you not to worry about your youngest daughter. She's going to be fine. God has great things in store for her and you can release your fears and anxiety about her."

Huh? Where'd *that* come from?

Just that morning, Bonnie and I had a long conversation about Elly, our youngest daughter, on this very subject. When I questioned George about it, he was baffled that I was baffled.

"Sometimes God prompts me to share something with others. I'm not always right, and I always share it gently as a 'sense' they need to pray about and confirm," he said. "But I've found that the more I act on those small promptings, the more I learn to distinguish God's voice."

In the years that followed, George became a close prayer partner and trusted friend. Occasionally he'd walk up to me, smiling and saying, "I've got a fun one . . ." and then tell me about some recent Spirit-led encounter. George lives with an awareness of God's presence in his daily life. He maintains that posture of receptivity we looked at in chapter 3. An untold number of people have their own versions of this type encounter with George, in which he spoke a specific and well-timed word of blessing.

Whether the speech is general wisdom or specific revelation, speaking in the prophetic way should always be oriented toward life. Our model is the creation story, which reveals how God speaks words into worlds and calls life out of chaos. Over the course of six days, God creates the world through a two-step process: separating and filling. God first separates things to create an ordered space for life. Once there's order, God then fills those spaces with life. He separates, then he fills.

The first three days are spent separating things—light from darkness, water from sky. The second three days are spent filling those ordered spaces with life—sun, moon, and stars; all kinds of living creatures. These days of separating and filling correlate with each other. After the three days of creation through separation, God returns on day four to where he started on day one. He fills the separated cosmos with the sun, moon, and stars. On day five, God returns to the space created on day two and populates the earth with animals.

The two-step process of creation—separating and filling—models how life is spoken into darkness and chaos. God separates what doesn't belong together, and he imparts new life into the voids. Life and death, blessing and cursing, are always before us (Deuteronomy 30:19). Words have the power to create new worlds by drawing us toward life.

A continual toast "To life"

Jewish people have long toasted, "To life!" *L'chaim*, which means "to/for life," is more than a nice sentiment for weddings or other celebrations, however. It names one of the central values of Judaism: life. You'll have a difficult time finding a bacon, egg, and cheese biscuit for breakfast in Jerusalem, because Jews who observe the kosher laws don't mix milk and meat. Milk is a symbol of life, and dead meat is death incarnate. You don't mix life and death. Death isn't even a thing in itself: it's the absence of life. Same for despair: it's the absence of hope. Death may come to you, and others may bring it to your doorstep, but you can always choose life. Moses's words in Deuteronomy 30:19—"Now choose life, so that you and

your children may live"—draw our minds to the creation story and orient us to the ways God speaks life into existence.

Our responsibility is to align our lives and speech to life, never to death or despair. Slander never has a place on our lips. It cuts through life. No matter how dark a place is, there's never a legitimate reason for despair. Our words can help distinguish and separate sources of life and death. We can admonish one another when we veer from life, but never as judge or with fatalism. Our words must always be oriented *l'chaim*.

Think about the power of life-giving words when we assume the posture of compassion with people in their suffering. When we love "as God has loved us" from the posture of compassion (proximity, solidarity, and emotional connectedness), we are poised to see new life in unexpected ways.

I caught a glimpse of it when I first met Stephanie and Kevin, the couple introduced in chapter 2. I later learned more about their story and how they first began dating, but at the time I met them they were already married.

After the last service on a Sunday morning, I was leaving the sanctuary and walking toward the parking lot when a young couple approached me. "Do you have a minute?" the man asked.

"Sure, what's going on?" I said. There was an awkward silence as they looked at each other.

Finally he said to her, "Do you want me to just tell him?" Stephanie lowered her head and didn't respond.

"We're getting divorced," Kevin said bluntly. "But I thought w should meet with a priest first, which they tell me is you in th type of church." He gave an embarrassed laugh and then shared little of the backstory. "She wasn't raised religious, but I'm Itali and went to mass as a kid and . . . I don't know. Well, I found y online. Do you have a few minutes to meet with us?"

This was a first for me. We went upstairs to my office and it immediately apparent that our meeting wasn't a last-ditch effor reconcile. It was more a means for Kevin to check off that last to appease his conscience and say, "We tried everything, inc ing 'divine intervention.'" He spoke first and with an air of

objectivity. The whole spiel was clearly a ruse. Stephanie didn't appear to care what he said and just wanted to get out of this awkward situation as soon as possible.

After Kevin finished, I looked to Stephanie, and she said, "He's a kid who said he was a man. He's a talker who can't say a single honest thing. He's cheated on me twice—that I know of. We have two kids, and we've had child services called on us. The more we need him, the faster he walks out the door."

I looked at Kevin, and he didn't say a word. Then, from her initially distant posture—which communicated "I'd like to be anywhere else in the world"—she began to share a gripping story, one that went from abandonment to hope and back to cruel abandonment. As Stephanie shared their story, a couple of tears ran down my cheek. I think I was more emotionally connected to Stephanie's story in the moment than she was, and my tears triggered emotions she didn't want to connect to. She stopped abruptly. "We'll be fine," she said. "We're fine."

Kevin then turned toward her and said, "I'm really sorry. I should have tried harder."

There was a pause. Then I spoke the first real words I had spoken during our session. I asked Kevin about the values driving his life. There was a clear disconnect between what he believed and how he was living.

By the end of the meeting, Kevin had made a lot of confessions and expressed considerable contrition. He agreed with Stephanie that divorce was inevitable. "Too much has happened," he said, and he accepted most of the responsibility. After a long pause that seemed to signal the end of the meeting—at which point they would walk out to their individual cars and head their separate ways—Stephanie looked at him for the first time. With tears streaming down her face, she said, "You broke every promise."

She gritted her teeth. "You knew . . ." she said, and then stopped and looked at me. She shook her head and winced. "Here's the thing. He's probably going to change, and someone else is going to benefit from the way he dragged us through hell. But it won't be us.

He'll abandon us. He's not going to be a father to these boys. He'll start a new family."

Stephanie looked back to him, "I wonder what the new and improved Kevin will be like." She reached down and started picking up her things. She stood to go.

"One question," I said. "Would you be willing to wait one week before filing for divorce, and have just one more meeting?"

"I don't think so," she said. But she didn't leave. She stood there in front of the door. I sensed an opportunity to carefully press in a little more.

"There's a counselor on our staff who specializes in helping couples with the aftermath of infidelity," I said. "After all you've been through, just one forty-five-minute meeting with him?"

She stood there shaking her head.

I pressed a bit deeper. "You probably aren't in this category, but a decent percentage of divorced people later say they wish they had leaned in a little more before the decision. A large percentage of couples who rank their marriages as absolutely miserable but choose to lean in rather than quit end up ranking their marriages as 'very good' five years later. How about one more meeting just to make sure?"

She looked at him. Kevin said, "I'd have another meeting."

Stephanie agreed to one more meeting, and they went their separate ways.

It's strange to reflect on that moment now, when she paused at the door. Today, their marriage is stronger than it's ever been. It was a messy journey, for sure, and one that is far from over. They even derailed a couple of times in the early stages, between stabilization and forgiveness and long before restoration. But they never threw in the towel for good. They chose to usher in new life.

If you ask Stephanie today why they ultimately never gave up, you'd hear about their spiritual conversion, the final forgiveness ceremony, Stephanie's healing journey, their counselor, and a few specific breakthrough moments along the way.

But one thread you'd pick up on that weaves through all of it is a woman named Babbitt. She was my wife's grandmother, and before she passed away, she did for Stephanie and Kevin what she had done for many others throughout her life. Stephanie and Kevin both say that without Babbitt, they probably wouldn't be married today. Who knows? But one thing is certain: the gift of radical hospitality Babbitt gave them is a powerful catalyst for new life.

Let's take a closer look.

HEALING PRESENCE

RADICAL HOSPITALITY

COLLECTIVE EMPOWERMENT

Part II

Radical Hospitality: Extend Your Family

7

Babbitt's Table

Babbitt" was our name for Bonnie's grandmother. The name has a long story, but basically, a three-year-old managed to rename his sixty-three-year-old grandmother, and it stuck.

Babbitt was a feisty, consummate nurturer. First, she would feed you. It wasn't a question. If you were a first-time guest and politely refused, she would put the plate down and say, "Oh, this is good. You need to eat more." Babbitt would scoot a chair next to you and lean in with a gentle smile. "So, what's the story? How's it going?" she'd say. If you tried to snow her, she'd put her hand on your arm or back and say, "C'mon, baby, what's going on?" You could be real with Babbitt. Babbitt's home was an extension of her life. Babbitt always had time for people. There was always a bed open and an extra seat at the table. For many adopted sons, daughters, grandsons, and granddaughters—including Stephanie and Kevin— her home was a simple, unchanging, nurturing environment that conveyed in a thousand ways: "You're always welcome here."

When Bonnie figuratively crash-landed during her sophomore year of college, she reached out to Babbitt. Hurt, ashamed, disillusioned, and needing a safe place to land, Bonnie picked up the phone and asked, "Can I stay with you for a while?"

"Of course. I'll make sure the room is ready," Babbitt said. Bonnie arrived to a big meal on the table, a bigger hug, a warm bed, and the greatest gift imaginable when you need to put the pieces back together: radical hospitality.

After a couple of days, Babbitt asked Bonnie, "So, what's the plan?" She was adept at sensing the line separating supporting and enabling. She wasn't afraid to pry into the messy details, but her goal was to help Bonnie relaunch. Her high instinct for nurture was matched with a tough love: "I love you, but I need to hurt your feelings for a moment . . ." With her hand on your back, she'd drop a truth bomb.

Babbitt was our first teacher in the school of radical hospitality.

What is radical hospitality?

Radical hospitality is the opening of our lives and homes to embrace a stranger as extended family. It's the soil where compassion flourishes. The word *hospitality* may call to mind the idea of entertaining guests at nicely decorated dinner parties, but it once meant embracing a stranger as family, even when it was inconvenient and the house was dirty. It's the high-level nurture, support, responsiveness, and availability that holds a family, neighborhood, and community together.

Radical doesn't mean "extreme," as many people assume; it means "core." Radical expressions of core commitments often appear extreme because they're rarely followed through in practice. But we misunderstand the distinction between an individual and collective calling when we view the faith and compassion of men and women who fully embody core commitments as a unique calling. Their expression is unique, but their level of obedience to God's voice is for all who respond.

We all need our basic needs met. But we need a Babbitt too. Right next to the need for clean water, good food, and decent shelter is the insatiable need to be uniquely and deeply known, heard, supported, touched, valued, understood, encouraged, enjoyed, and believed in.

This is what Babbitt did so well. She built a safe nest and was ready to step in when you needed a mama. Imagine losing your way and needing a safe place to land. If you were alone and hungry, you'd be grateful for a food pantry. But what would you give to be able to pick up the phone and know that a Babbitt was there and glad to have you? She might serve you some of the same food you'd get at a food pantry, but it would be a completely different meal.

Babbitt's gift of hospitality had some specific qualities that magnified its impact. Babbitt had an easy smile, but the deep lines on her face betrayed a difficult past. She possessed a feisty optimism, like a small winch that could pull out a vehicle completely buried in the mud. It was birthed when she was abandoned by her mother as a child and quit school to become a mother for her younger siblings. "There's always a way; we just need to find it," she'd often say. It was true for a convicted felon, "a nice fella who just needs a second chance," and it was true for chocolate brownies without a mix. If she discovered you liked chocolate, she was known to deep-freezer-dive for half-eaten Easter bunnies to melt down into brownies. Politely and persuasively, Babbitt would keep moving forward with a disarming smile that didn't fully conceal her indomitable spirit.

Babbitt also held tightly to the idea that nothing needs to be wasted. It was true for aluminum foil and leftovers and it was true for the pain in our past. There's always potential for redemption and a reason for hope. A person in his or her worst moment should never become frozen in our minds. Even when that person is us.

The willingness to inconvenience yourself for others is a priceless gift. For Babbitt, it had become a normal part of life. You just put people first. You leave space. You learn how to turn strangers into extended family members who quickly feel at home.

It strikes me that these few pages are the most words ever written about Babbitt. There was never an article written about her compassionate exploits or how she influenced an untold number of family generations and individual legacies. Babbitt was unremarkably and yet decisively influential for many families. Her gift of hospitality was the kind of glue that holds a family, neighborhood, and community together.

Babbitt's funeral was one of the single most inspiring events I've ever attended. A long funeral probably seems like a nightmare, but hers was like a cross between a Tony Robbins conference and an enjoyable family reunion of biologically unrelated people. Babbitt's massive network of adopted sons and daughters told crazy, funny stories, with the constant theme of life and her way of bringing it out. Age didn't increase her rigidity, skepticism, or fears. She was a lover of people, and she never gave up hope.

Some of the stories were stranger than fiction. Her sister went to prison for murdering her husband on a drunken binge. They were both drunk, and no one will ever know what really happened. Babbitt took in her niece and cared for her sister when she was released. At the same time, she was mourning the death of her own daughter and caring for a young mother in the aftermath of domestic violence who had no extended family.

Was she ever burned? Sure. Did people disappoint her? Of course. Was she a hot mess in her own right? She'd just smile at the question. But her late husband would tell of the time he renovated the kitchen despite her repeated objections to his plan. He came home one afternoon to find Babbitt wielding heavy machinery and ripping out the new cabinets. "Cleave, I told you they wouldn't work, and this is my kitchen."

Was she tempted to become cynical, give up on people, or turn inward to the problems and pain at home? Strangely, no. That afternoon at her funeral, a mixed bag of people, of all ages and races, connected only by their intersection with Babbitt, came to give tribute. Together, we found ourselves in an unexpected front-row seat to one of the most influential forces for new life: radical hospitality. Babbitt was many things, but mostly she was *there*.

One of the greatest gifts we can give our communities is the gift of extended family. Our communities need ten thousand acts of authentic compassion that are well networked and responsive to real needs. We need ten thousand Babbitts who say things like, "Food pantries are good, but where we can, let's try to move people into our kitchens"; "Baby, what's the real story?"; "He's a nice fella who needs a second chance." We need people who put others first, leave space, and turn strangers into extended family members who quickly feel at home.

Reconfiguring the ordinary

This core practice of radical hospitality is biblical and impactful, but it is also highly countercultural for many of us in the western world. Putting people first, leaving space, and extending family to strangers is difficult when we're never home and running at breakneck speed. A related but maybe less obvious barrier to hospitality is simply how we view our homes.

I have long viewed our home as a sanctuary. You could get me to embrace the idea of tangential hospitality, but there was a firewall at the front door of *mi casa*. Life is full throttle and chaotic, so our home needed to be a respite and recharging station for us. Dinner parties were carefully scheduled and capped at two hours.

Then we met Wendy Vernon. She's a "British Babbitt," of sorts, and she really messed up our view of home and hospitality, especially as it related to children and families in crisis and transition. I first met with Wendy and Paul Vernon one evening in my office, when they scheduled an appointment to learn more about our foster care initiatives as a church. The Vernons were members of our church, and I assumed they were interested in participating in one of the ministries we had highlighted at a recent weekend service.

So on that evening, this couple—both in their mid-sixties, with thick British accents—showed up with a loaf of freshly baked bread and three infants they were fostering. Paul took a crying infant out of a car seat as we sat down. "This is our retirement," he said with a smile. Wendy, with her purple highlights and pretense-free manner of speaking, started out with a series of questions that clearly revealed their passion for kids from hard places and their knowledge of the system. Then she said, "We help coordinate the foster care licensing classes and would like to host some here at the church. Would that be okay?" We agreed. Only later did I discover that Wendy and Paul are tireless advocates for foster care who sit on state and local boards addressing policy and practice issues, including helping the dependency court launch a pilot "baby court" program in Lee County, Florida.

Before I met the Vernons, I would have expected a conversation between Wendy and someone considering fostering children to go something like this:

Person or couple on the fence: *I'm interested in getting involved, but am not sure it's the right time.*

Wendy: *What are your reservations?*

On the fence: *I'm afraid I don't have the time these kids will need.*

Wendy: *Yeah, it's a major commitment that isn't for everybody, and you shouldn't just jump into it.*

On the fence: *I also don't think my heart could stand letting them go back home.*

Wendy: *That's one of the hardest things about foster care. It's definitely something God will need to call you to do. If you're not called to it and if it's not the right time for your family, it won't work.*

On the fence: *Thanks for not pressuring or guilting me into it! That's really refreshing. I'll spend some more time praying and doing research.*

Conversations never go this way with Wendy. Instead, her innocent and disarming "drive-by guiltings" go something like this:

Person or couple on the fence: *I'm interested in fostering, but am not sure it's the right time.*

Wendy: *Why not?*

On the fence: *I'm afraid I don't have the time these kids will need.*

Wendy: *We don't either, but we figured they'd prefer joining our mess to living in a group home.*

On the fence (taken aback by the phrase "group home"): *Well, I don't think my heart could stand letting them leave after we bonded.*

Wendy (smiling because she's heard this a thousand times and enjoys creating an awkward moment here): *You think I don't have a heart?*

On the fence (smiling back, somewhat embarrassed): *No . . . I mean . . . I'm just not sure I'm cut out for it. I'm also waiting for confirmation from God to make sure it's the right thing.*

Wendy: *Oh, well you've got that already. That's the good news. It's a scriptural mandate to care for orphans, and these are our orphans.*

On the fence: *I don't know that I agree that everyone should be foster parents.*

Wendy: *I don't either. But these aren't reasons to say no. If those were good reasons, the four hundred thousand kids in foster care would be resigned to group homes, and we can't let that happen. The church must give these kids a home.*

On the fence: *How do you know it won't disrupt your family?*

Wendy (laughing): *Disrupt your family! They'll turn it upside down! They'll stretch you in ways you can't imagine! But it probably needs to happen anyway—and you'll get to help a child who will make you more like Jesus. It's a win for everybody.*

People squirm, get frustrated, and occasionally grow annoyed, but they can't dismiss Wendy. She has this type of conversation with a baby in one arm and two other children standing by her side.

Part of my surprise at first was the missing motivational tone or nuance when discussing such a major life commitment. "Wendy, wouldn't it be more helpful to soften the edges and accentuate the bright spots?" I wanted to ask her. "It's just not as simple as you make it out to be."

She just doesn't see it that way. Wendy seeks to normalize what is often viewed as exceptional. She doesn't understand why the decision to foster has to be so complicated. To her, it is a no-brainer: if a child needs a home, you move heaven and earth to find one. To this day, it is unconscionable to her that tens of thousands of kids are waiting to be adopted and that churches far outnumber the children. She doesn't get it. You put people first—especially kids! You make room. You reprioritize where necessary. It may seem exceptional, but it should be normal. These conversations are Wendy's way of following Jesus' unconventional method of motivating the disciples to go out "like sheep among wolves" (Matthew 10:16). It's just what we do. Just because it isn't commonly practiced doesn't mean it shouldn't be. Anytime someone tries to elevate Wendy to superhuman status or interpret her and Paul's choice as a unique calling, Wendy is quick to say, "Oh, no, we're not special. We just said yes."

The practice of radical hospitality can happen in many different arenas and not always via foster care, but no matter the form it takes, radical hospitality is simply part of following Jesus. Putting people first, leaving space, and finding ways to turn strangers into extended family members are integral parts of embodying God's kingdom in our communities.

When you speak so plainly about countercultural ideas, it forces people to wrestle with their worldviews and assumptions. But Wendy is far from an idealistic dreamer disconnected from the real world. I distinctly remember one night, around week three of fostering the twins, when Bonnie was at a breaking point. I stepped outside and called Wendy. "I'm not sure what to do," I told her. "My wife is about to lose her mind, and I seriously think we over-committed. We're no match for these girls."

Wendy came right over, with two kids in tow, and sat with us for a couple of hours. She was empathetic, reassuring, and practically helpful. She laughed as Bonnie told her that one of the girls had thrown a dirty diaper across the room and yelled, "Poo party, poo party!" while her sister cheered her on. Wendy called a behavioral specialist for us the next day and checked on Bonnie a couple of times that week. The Vernons did the same for many others as they sought to build a rich network of support both within and for foster families.

The case for authoritative communities

What the Vernons are doing for children in southwest Florida is what an increasing number of researchers suggest our communities need more than anything. The Vernons and others like them are building a rich community of individuals and families responding to immediate needs with high levels of nurture and support. Today, if you foster children in southwest Florida, you can find a vibrant community to help you that didn't exist several years ago. You can quickly learn whom to call for an education- or health-related question. If you need behavioral support, you can get the referral within a couple of days. This little community the Vernons helped build is both cohesive and flexible. The Vernons would be quick to name scores of others who are instrumental in the work, and they would say that there is still much work to be done. But the *type* of work they've done for children is what I want to highlight.

At first, the Vernons had to learn how the system worked and who could help with what needs. They learned where the gaps were and worked with others to help fill them. There was a huge learning curve. What are the needs? What are the assets? Where are the service gaps? Who needs to help in what areas? Their approach to helping children was highly relational and strategic.

The Commission on Children at Risk, a panel of leading children's doctors, research scientists, and youth service professionals, published a report entitled *Hardwired to Connect: The New Scientific Case for Authoritative Communities*.[1] This report details the need for new strategies to address the unprecedented struggles kids in the United States are facing. After citing ominous research on the decreasing physical and mental health of children in the United States, the researchers elevate two key problems we must address in our communities: our waiting lists are too long, and our intellectual models are inadequate.

Too many kids are struggling, and we need a better response. From the commission's perspective, the most effective response would be the strengthening of "authoritative communities" around children. Basically, we need communities full of Babbitts: friends, neighbors, teachers, pastors, and coaches who consistently support children with high levels of nurture and high boundaries. The commission's recommendations are based on empirical evidence and center on the observation that children are biologically "hardwired" for enduring attachments to other people and for moral and spiritual meaning. These attachments are prerequisites for a child's healthy development, yet they are weakening in many of our communities.

The commission's proposal is to build "authoritative communities" in our neighborhoods, defined by the following characteristics:

1. Treat children as ends in themselves
2. Extend warmth and nurture
3. Establish clear limits and expectations
4. Perform most of the work by nonspecialists
5. Work multigenerationally
6. Maintain a long-term focus
7. Reflect and transmit what it means to be a good person
8. Encourage spiritual and religious development
9. Remain philosophically oriented to the equal dignity of all persons and to the principle of love of neighbor[2]

One specific example of these principles at work is the Communities That Care model. It's a five-phase change process that draws on the latest research in prevention science and is demonstrating fantastic results across the United States, including a more-than-fivefold return on investment. The five phases are as follows: get started, get organized, develop a community profile, create a plan, and implement and evaluate. The Vernons weren't aware of the model, but it's exactly what they did. And it's what our communities need more than anything.

The qualitative aspects of the commission's report are intriguing for such a broad panel of experts. Kids need moral and spiritual meaning. They need to be taught what "goodness" entails. They need high expectations and firm boundaries. They need warmth and consistent nurture. They need adults in the community to support the work in the home. What our communities need to flourish are, in many ways, the same qualities our families need to flourish.

Lessons from family systems theory
In the 1960s, Diana Baumrind, a developmental psychologist, suggested that healthy parenting styles blend two characteristics: responsiveness and demandingness. High degrees of nurture and structure are held together in a consistent and responsive way. Parents who emphasize structure (demandingness) to the detriment of nurture are authoritarian. They're often too harsh or rigid. On the other side is the permissive style, which is characterized by high responsiveness and low structure. Boundaries are absent. The sweet

spot for Baumrind is the authoritative style, which blends high degrees of structure and nurture. *Auctor*, the Latin root of the word *authoritative*, means "one who creates." In Baumrind's research on parenting styles, an authoritative approach, with a consistent, responsive, and high level of nurture and structure, creates the best conditions for children to thrive.

The same is true for our communities. We need more Vernons to build the relational networks that can respond to individuals and families in need with a good blend of nurture and structure. One of the greatest gifts we can give our communities is the gift of extended family: ten thousand acts of authentic compassion that are well networked and responsive to real needs. When we put people first, leave space, and learn to turn strangers into extended family members, we'll see new life rise up all around us.

Five practices of radical hospitality

What about you? How might you begin to open your life and home in more intentional ways and recover the practice of radical hospitality? Building on the principles of love, listen, discern, and respond, these chapters in part 2 will introduce you to some perspectives and practices that can help you discern how to best embody the value of radical hospitality. We'll use the acronym BREAD to describe the five practices of radical hospitality.

- Begin with *xenia*
- Recruit mentors
- Embrace tension
- Allow margin
- Discern *kairos*

We'll unfold these practices in the next chapter, beginning with an all-important paradigm shift for us in the Western Hemisphere.

8

Boundaries and Your Capacity for Chaos

How radical is radical enough? How deep does the call to hospitality and compassion need to go? How much should one make sure to keep? How much to give away?

These questions came to my mind a few years ago when we attended our first national orphan summit. It was like a microcosm of heaven. We met so many families who embodied an otherworldly set of values like the Vernons. A caseworker and father of three stood on the stage with a teenager who had been adopted before aging out of the system. The caseworker spoke about God's heart for the orphan. He had worked with the teenage girl to put together her life book for adoption, which would introduce her to prospective families. Many months passed, and no one stepped forward with even the slightest interest. Just before she was set to be emancipated from the system, her caseworker called and said, "Great news! There's a family interested in adopting you, and I think they're a perfect match." She had already resigned herself to being on her own, so the call caught her off guard. "Who? What are they like? Will I have any siblings?"

"Hold on," her caseworker said. "We'll be there in thirty minutes. You can ask them. But I think it's a perfect match."

He arrived a few minutes before the family and helped the girl get ready. Then, while she stepped into the bathroom, her caseworker slipped out into the lobby. When she walked out, he was standing there with his own family. They were holding a large banner that read "Welcome to our family!" Her first name and their last name was printed in all caps.

To hear this young woman speak about what it has meant to her to be grafted into her caseworker's family—well, it was like a front-row seat to heaven. Her story made you want to run out into the halls of every church and grab all your friends until every one of the kids waiting to be adopted in your state or province can echo her story.

So many families at the conference had their own version of the Vernons' story. They just said yes. They made space. They prioritized people. Radical hospitality became a normal way of life.

Their choices have a prophetic edge to them. It isn't just that they are running in a different lane than most of us; they are running a different race. At the conference, many of the stories told messed with me, because they were confronting me with a different life paradigm. Sometimes these stories inspired me, and other times they made me feel defensive. Sometimes they even evoked concern. "Wow, you're fostering five kids in addition to your two biological kids?" I'd say. Left unsaid: "Are you sure that's a good idea? Aren't you overcommitted?"

Some of these families practiced such radical hospitality that it seemed there were no boundaries in sight and that they were headed for a quick burnout—or worse, maybe even setting their children up for serious problems down the road. I remember joking with Bonnie once after a local foster parent banquet that the "foster parent of the year" award was a death sentence. It was given to the family who survived against everyone's expectations. "Wow! They're still standing? We should give them an award, because at this rate they may not make it to next year's banquet." Stories of their impact on kids would be shared that were often prefaced with the recounting of a conversation like this:

Agency representative: *We have a group of seven siblings who need a home tonight. Can you take them?*

Family: *No, sorry; we already have five. We're actually at our legal max.*

Agency: *We can give you a temporary waiver.*

Family: *I don't think we can do it.*

Agency: *Okay, we understand.*

Family: *Where will you send them?*

Agency: *We'll split them apart into different group homes.*

Family: *Just bring them here. We'll figure it out. Twelve kids in an eighteen-hundred-square-foot home? No problem!*

Foster parents of the year!

I continue to wrestle with questions such as, "How radical is radical enough?" "How deep does the call to hospitality and compassion need to go?" It's good and appropriate to wrestle with the tension between hospitality and boundaries. How should we do it? What is there to learn from those who have done it best? Let's take a look at the "bread" of radical hospitality: the core practices that bring it to life.

Begin with *xenia*

Xenos is the Greek word for "guest." In the ancient world, *xenia* (hospitality) was a well-structured expectation. It was also sacred space. *Theoxeny—theo + xenia*, or "hospitality of/with God"— was a theme in Greek writings in which people extend hospitality to a stranger and later find out that the stranger was a disguised god. Hebrews 13:2 says, "Do not forget to show hospitality to strangers, for by so doing some people have shown hospitality to angels without knowing it." Jesus himself said, "Whatever you did for one of the least of these brothers and sisters of mine, you did for me" (Matthew 25:40). Such stories and teachings reinforce the importance of *xenia*.

If stories of *theoxeny* weren't sufficiently motivating, stories like Sodom and Gomorrah, the Trojan War, and Cyclops remind us of the consequences of breaking *xenia*. Cyclops has one eye because he tried to eat rather than welcome Odysseus. Just your everyday feel-good bedtime story: "Son, you don't do that to guests. If you don't want to be a Cyclops, practice hospitality!"

Fast-forward a bit to the Roman Empire. By this point, the practice of hospitality in the early church was widespread but limited to individual homes because of persecution. Jesus had clearly established the practices of extending hospitality to strangers, healing the sick, and caring for the marginalized for his followers. It's just what you do. It's not a special calling; it's part of the basic package when you say yes to Jesus. You embrace those who are marginalized and you cure diseases, which often meant embracing those with diseases.

This message was not lost on the early church. Accounts of the early church's response to epidemics reveal the common and widespread practice of hospitality, even in the face of potential death, as a core element of their faith. There could be no hospital in such a setting. Rather, the hospital was the home and small dorms close by.

After emperor Constantine's conversion to Christianity, the practice of hospitality took on a larger and more centralized dimension. The church grew quickly, but so did poverty and disease. In Cappadocia in the 300s, Saint Basil constructed what would later be called a "Basilias," which was basically a city of healing.[1] It was an area with hospitals for patients suffering from different illnesses; homes, offices, and schools for doctors and nurses; and all the basic infrastructure required to support it. Saint Gregory of Nazianzus called it "an easy ascent to heaven." This Basilias became a model throughout the Christian church, and soon others were built in Alexandria, Ephesus, and Constantinople. Wherever possible, the Basilica (church) was to have a Basilias next door. Where such structures proved unfeasible, small groups of Christians built *xenodochiums*, which were homes for the poor, sick, and orphaned. Like Jesus, when the church went into new areas, they did two things: they healed and they taught. All in the context of radical hospitality.

May it happen again! May the full healing ministry of Jesus be reclaimed in his church! And may the radical hospitality that undergirds it move from a special calling for a few to a common practice for all who follow Jesus.

Recruit mentors

The second practice in radical hospitality is to recruit mentors. Your mentors will likely change what you do. Churchill's quote comes to mind: "We shape our buildings; thereafter, they shape us." Mentors provide a relational support structure. Because radical hospitality is a countercultural practice, it's essential to build a community of people around us who reflect the values we most want to embody.

Drafting behind mentors, as a runner closely follows another to avoid wind resistance, has a way of calibrating our life choices in so many vital but seemingly small ways. The Vernons never said a word about any of this, but they had a role to play in decisions Bonnie and I made about specific purchases and weekend activities, and even in our perspective on retirement. We've decided that we don't want to ever fully retire. Paul wasn't kidding when he said, "This is our retirement." They have quite a ministry with the sixty-plus demographic: people who are looking for a compelling vision for how to spend themselves well at their stage of life. They offer a compelling alternative to the common "I sacrificed all those years; now it's 'me time'" approach to retirement.

One side note: imagine the impact on our communities if ageism and self-indulgent retirement pursuits were replaced with an honoring of our elderly and a sacrificial approach to generativity. In my experience, most people over sixty have a strong desire to influence and serve younger generations. Erik Erikson's stages of life development identify the tension at this stage as "generativity versus stagnation." When a person has a fair amount of money and time, stagnation isn't as bad as it sounds: "I may not be using most of my time, wisdom, and resources to influence future generations, but it feels really good to sit beside the pool and relax." When you couple the prevailing ideas of retirement with the perplexing obsession with youth, it sets our communities up for a disadvantage.

Why would we let our greatest repositories of wisdom, time, and resources pursue blissful stagnation without a fight? It's one thing if they're making an intentional choice. But many wander into that territory because of a lack of a viable alternative. In the communities I've worked with most closely, it seems a lot of wisdom, time, and resources simply aren't connected to the most pressing struggles facing the communities. The retired folks are off somewhere else, and often they're not even sought after other than by their own families. If this is an accurate depiction of your context, I'd encourage you to investigate it some more. As a pastor in south Florida, I was able to see firsthand the impact of intergenerational collaboration on pressing challenges, and I can tell you: it's worth the effort to repair any real or perceived disconnect between older folks who can serve as mentors and those in your community.

Returning to the larger idea of mentoring and the pursuit of radical hospitality: When we surround ourselves with people who reflect the values we most want to embody, it provides a far sturdier scaffolding for our growth than what we'd find within our own minds. You can attend a meeting like the orphan summit and be moved to action, but by the time the teachings run through your filters and you reenter familiar routines, the actual impact may come out more like fat-free ice cream than the real thing. It may have the same name and a familiar look, but it's not the same thing by that point. The same goes for the isolated pursuit of radical hospitality in a highly individualistic and consumer-oriented society. It probably won't happen on its own. Radical hospitality is a different way of living than our society naturally sets us up for, and time with good mentors can reorient our perspective to God's kingdom and help move our good intentions into core practices.

In addition to spending time with personal mentors, one practice I've found exceedingly helpful is reading biographies of people, particularly from different places and times, who embody the traits I want to cultivate. Men like William Passavant, George Muller, and Jean Vanier and women like Mathilda Wrede, Cornelia Bonnell, and Jane Addams are in my head. They help me question my assumptions and the ideas I naturally accept as givens. They influence my engagement with Scripture and challenge my faith.

In the biography of Hudson Taylor, *Hudson Taylor's Spiritual Secret*, the following account is told in the first person, based on his journal:

After concluding my last service about ten o'clock that night, a poor man asked me to go and pray with his wife, saying that she was dying. I readily agreed, and on the way asked him why he had not sent for the priest, as his accent told me he was an Irishman. He had done so, he said, but the priest refused to come without a payment of eighteen pence, which the man did not possess as the family was starving. Immediately it occurred to my mind that all the money I had in the world was the solitary half-crown, and that it was in one coin; moreover, that while the basin of water-gruel I usually took for supper was awaiting me, and there was sufficient in the house for breakfast in the morning, I certainly had nothing for dinner on the coming day.

I little dreamed that the truth of the matter simply was that I could trust God plus one-and-sixpence, but was not prepared to trust Him only, without any money at all in my pocket.

Up a miserable flight of stairs into a wretched room he led me, and oh, what a sight there presented itself! Four or five children stood about, their sunken cheeks and temples telling unmistakably the story of slow starvation, and lying on a wretched pallet was a poor, exhausted mother, with a tiny infant thirty-six hours old moaning rather than crying at her side. "Ah!" thought I, "if I had two shillings and a sixpence, instead of half-a-crown, how gladly should they have one-and-sixpence of it." But still a wretched unbelief prevented me from obeying the impulse to relieve their distress at the cost of all I possessed. It will scarcely seem strange that I was unable to say much to comfort these poor people. I needed comfort myself. I began to tell them, however, that they must not be cast down; that though their circumstances were very distressing there was a kind and loving Father in heaven. But something within me cried, "You hypocrite! telling these unconverted people about a kind and loving Father in heaven, and not prepared yourself to trust Him without half-a-crown."

"You asked me to come and pray with your wife," I said to the man; "let us pray." And I knelt down. But no sooner had I opened my lips with, "Our Father who art in heaven," than conscience said within, "Dare you mock God? Dare you kneel down and call Him 'Father' with that half-crown in your pocket?"

Not only was the poor woman's life saved, but my life as I fully realized had been saved too.

The very next morning, I received an envelope. On opening the envelope I found nothing written within, but inside a sheet of blank paper was folded a pair of kid gloves from which, as I opened them in astonishment, half-a-sovereign fell to the ground.[2]

The half sovereign was over ten times what he had given away! Hudson Taylor couldn't see the chain of events this act of faithfulness would set into motion, but in a few months he would be asked to quit his medical program and, without funds, embark on a dangerous five-month voyage to interior China, an area engaged in a civil war that no missionary had visited before. He would go on to spend fifty-one years in China and lead a mission society that would bring over eight hundred missionaries to China, start 125 schools, see eighteen thousand conversions to Christianity, and establish more than three hundred stations of work across all eighteen provinces. And about that single event, he would later write, "I cannot tell you how often my mind has recurred to this incident, or all the help it has been to me in circumstances of difficulty. If we are faithful to God in little things, we shall gain experience and strength that will be helpful to us in the more serious trials."[3]

These types of stories are like a dose of pure oxygen for those living under heavy smog. One of Taylor's quotations—"God's work done God's way will never lack God's supply"—is before me each day as a subtle but constant reorientation to God's kingdom.

A few years ago, our congregation was at a critical juncture with the medical center we were building, and we experienced a major setback that made it seem almost impossible to move forward. We had sensed God's leading for a long time, and that didn't change when the setback occurred. But it certainly evoked a lot of fear and led us to entertain all sorts of compromises to the vision. Taylor's story, and others like it, provided some much-needed insulation to protect us from a practical agnosticism.

When you choose to embody radical hospitality, it's important to jump into the lane with people already running in it well. Hopefully, some of those people can be close by and accessible for conversation and prayer. Others may only be present through their writings. Overall, you'll find that the more you expose yourself to people like the Vernons and to writings like Taylor's, the more you will orient and align your life to God's kingdom.

Embrace tension

Along with the role of good mentors is the need to apply the right amount of tension for growth. A young couple without children once said yes to adopting a sibling group of seven. "Love is enough," they said. Love is often enough to *say* yes, but it's not always enough to carry it through wholeheartedly until completion. These children were in loving and long-term foster homes with families willing to adopt them. After prayer and conversation with these families, the couple decided to foster a sibling pair under age five instead, and it was a much better match.

When it comes to the tension between hospitality and boundaries, it's helpful to think about how tension produces growth. There's no growth without tension, but tension must be wisely calibrated. Somewhere between atrophy and being torn apart is a good stretching. Full immersive experiences have their place, and every faith journey brings us to chasms where we jump or we don't jump. There are no baby steps across a chasm. But in general, growth is a process of being slowly and consistently stretched.

Peter Senge, author of *The Fifth Discipline*, describes healthy tension with this metaphor: Imagine you hold your hands together, one on top of the other, and you place small rubber bands around each set of fingers. As you pull your hands apart, you begin to feel the tension. There's no tension at a place of rest. But if you quickly pull your hands apart and rip off the rubber bands, you no longer have tension either. Tension must be wisely calibrated.

Another young twentysomething couple without kids, who were interested in fostering, took a different route. As soon as they completed their licensing classes, the agency asked if they would consider fostering a sixteen-year-old girl. They said yes, and several months later they adopted her. It's an unorthodox family, with only nine years between parents and child, but it was a decision they felt God clearly leading them to make, and they're doing extremely well. We always want to give space for God to transcend our wisdom and stretch us beyond our perceived limits. But barring God's

direct leading, we can grow within this tension between hospitality and boundaries by starting small; exercising wisdom based on
expert opinion, best practices, and the feedback of mentors; and
slowly building on successes.

Love shifts boundaries

Starting small, drawing on good wisdom, and building on
successes are three ways to consistently apply the right amount
of tension for growth. But not just any growth. We're pursuing
growth in loving as Jesus loves. The reason we extend our families
and open our homes to strangers is because we love as Jesus loves.
He set an example for us and said, "Do as I have done" (John
13:15) and "You will be blessed if you do" (John 13:17).

Love, by its nature, expands our boundaries. It doesn't eviscer-
ate them; it widens them. Patience, one of the qualities of love,
is boundary shifting. "Normally, my fuse would run out by this
point," I sometimes think. "But God's love has changed me, and
the fuse is continually doused with God's grace." The same is true
of kindness, long-suffering, and the protecting, trusting, hoping,
and preserving acts of love. They enlarge our natural boundaries.

But what helps love preserve and establish healthy boundaries in
the right places? Truth. Truth and love function together as the best
fulcrum for radical hospitality. Together, they help us manage our
yeses and nos. In the same way that healthy parenting requires high
degrees of support and nurture (that is, appropriate boundaries
and unconditional love), the wise extension of radical hospitality
requires truth and love.

In the weeks after Robin's treatment, she faced a tough decision.
How anonymous would she be about her illness and recovery? She
was willing to share her story if it might help someone, but people
encouraged her to keep it secret. Her son encouraged her to risk
vulnerability. "You'll help people for sure, but I think it will also be
a part of your redemptive story as well." His affirmation confirmed
what she felt in her spirit.

Robin started to share the chronicles of her recovery journey on
social media and then put together a blog as soon as she completed
treatment. People contacted her. A lot of people. Many applauded

her, some asked for help with their own situations, and a few told her to stop talking about her recovery. But she would not stop. "I've already helped too many people," she responds confidently. "At first it was hard. This guy from my church contacted me and told me to focus on my recovery and stop sharing my journey. I asked a lot of people, including my therapists, about this advice. My therapists were actually reading my posts and they told me it was cathartic, and encouraged me to continue."

A few blog posts later, Robin now speaks with women from all over the United States every day. Recently, her phone number was given to a girl in a homeless shelter in Utah who needed help. Robin passed the number on to another woman, who received free transportation and a cash deposit for addiction treatment from several of Robin's friends who came together with their funds. A clearer view of the need and a couple of powerful success stories have led Robin to share her story more publicly and engage in advocacy work on all levels. Women suffering life-controlling addictions find far more than a testimony in Robin. They find extended family and a safe place to begin a healing journey.

Could your home be a similar safe place? Where could you begin to open your life and extend your home to embrace a stranger as extended family? What might radical hospitality look like in this season of life? For Robin, radical hospitality means embracing women facing life-controlling addictions. For Bonnie and me and our family, it means giving a home to kids from hard places. Who is it for you? A single mother you keep bumping into? A person God keeps placing on your mind? A couple in a strained marriage? Someone needing to get back on his feet and find a job? A refugee family?

It's true: we can't say yes to everything, and it's important to get our yeses right.

Every yes is ten thousand nos.

Too many yeses is a no-yes.

A half-hearted yes is a disguised no.

A presumptuous yes is a no to the right yes.

When you're presented with a specific opportunity to practice radical hospitality, what should you say? The very same boundaries can be established out of self-absorption or a clear sense of purpose. The very same openness to radical hospitality can come from deep deficits or deep love. Such yeses and nos can look the same on the outside, but it's important to distinguish between them. What is the difference between this boundary-shifting love and becoming a doormat for anyone to walk over?

In intimate relationships, it's common to identify a threshold at which someone with healthy levels of love and concern begins to malfunction and take on unhealthy codependent qualities. The story of Bill and Lois Wilson, founders of Alcoholics Anonymous and Al-Anon, as told in the film *When Love Is Not Enough*, describes the process well. Lois's enabling behaviors helped to perpetuate Bill's alcoholism. When he finally began to manage his disease without her help, it left her feeling neglected and resentful. His addiction had permeated their family system, and they each were playing a role.

When we practice radical hospitality, we invite a certain amount of stress into our family system. It's good to be mindful of this impact. Stress is tension, which is essential for growth, but there are certainly thresholds where growth ceases and fractures begin.

When a family lived with us for a couple of months, there were all sorts of dynamics we had to sort through. Was it okay for the sweaty preteen to sit in "my chair" and eat Doritos? The sight raised my heart rate. How would we respond to our young son crying that one of their kids threw one of his favorite Lego sets off a second-floor balcony? Our families had different expectations in many areas, and both individually and collectively we had to contend with our thresholds. Is this frustration a sign that love needs to supplant selfishness in an area, or is it a legitimate boundary that needs reinforcing?

Are we healthy enough to expand our boundaries?

I remember a conversation we had with the Vernons before we agreed to foster children. "I feel like we already walk on the precipice of chaos," I said. "Some children with high needs will probably knock us over the edge. I think you guys just have a higher threshold for chaos than we do."

Bonnie smiled at me. I qualified my statement: "Well . . . than *I* do."

On the continuum between rigid and flexible, the Vernons were on the far side of flexible. I wondered if those qualities were more important than they intimated in their advocacy for children. Should a more rigid family system like ours—with a high degree of structure and a low tolerance for disorder or surprises—foster children who would clearly turn it upside down? We have friends who both have obsessive-compulsive disorder. A "poo party" would be the end of them.

It's helpful to take a close look at our family system when we stretch toward radical hospitality. Where should we stretch, and how quickly? The circumplex model, established by David Olson, author of the popular marriage resource Prepare/Enrich, is a great place to start.[4]

Similar to Baumrind's work on parenting styles, the circumplex model suggests that healthy family systems share two traits in common: cohesiveness and adaptability. Cohesiveness refers to the level of emotional bonding in the family. It's the glue that holds everyone together. The glue can be weak, or it can be so strong that there's no elasticity to it. Adaptability refers to the level of change a family can tolerate. Both cohesiveness and adaptability function as continuums from low to high, where the poles are the trouble spots. From low to high, the continuum for adaptability moves from rigid to structured to flexible to chaotic. The continuum for cohesiveness moves from enmeshed to connected to separated to disengaged. Every family leans toward one side or the other on both of these continuums.

Healthy families are by no means identical, but in their own way they manage an openness to change with a cohesive identity as a family. Think of the model as a motion picture more than a static image. How does your family respond to changes? To what degree can it absorb disruptions and stress? How would your family respond to them? Our culture, background, personalities, life stages, and commitments all affect the dynamics of our family system. As we think about how and where to stretch ourselves toward radical hospitality, it's good to do so within the context of our particular family system.

Here's another way to think about it. The Royal Family Kids Camp, a summer camp for foster youth, has a ratio of one counselor to two campers. The counselors and support staff are able to create a safe, highly structured, and nurturing environment for these children. There is enough love present to absorb the pain. They're able to flex and deal with outbursts and meltdowns without the whole camp being hijacked. If the same camp had a ratio of one counselor to ten campers, it would not achieve the same results. It may have the same vision, strategy, commitment, and passion, but the desired culture and environment would likely be overwhelmed by the needs of the children.

The same pain that a healthy family system can absorb from others can exacerbate the existing struggles in a more fragile or toxic family. Had we fostered the twins when our three biological children were ages five, three, and one, the results would have been far different. All seven of us would have signaled "Mayday!" A few years later, when our children were older, it was a different story.

As you look outside and look within, where are the best and wisest opportunities to begin extending your family and opening your home? If your family is on the far end of one of these continuums, starting small and slow will be important. You don't need to wait until the conditions are perfect—you just need to be a bit more on the side of healthy than of fragile. Mentors who know you well can give you a green light. If you lean toward rigidity, you'll need to be honest and realistic about your threshold for chaos and to find ways to slowly expand your boundaries. If you have young children and work occupies a lot of time, you'll need to be creative to find ways to naturally connect with others in existing time frames and spaces. If your family is moderately healthy and you spend a decent amount of time and energy on the pursuit of happiness, you probably have a lot to offer and just need to find the best ways to draw others into your life and home.

Together, recovering the biblical practice of *xenia*, recruiting and drafting behind good mentors, and embracing a healthy amount of tension are ways to grow toward radical hospitality, which is the seedbed of smart compassion.

But what if you simply don't have time for any of it?

9

Hospitality from an Eternal Perspective

In 2012 I was working on a project that took me around the world to interview experts on science and religion. At the top of my list for one of the segments was an interview with a University of Oxford mathematician named John Lennox. We had interviewed a twentysomething agnostic who was intrigued by John's writings, and I knew that a personal interview with John would be an excellent addition to the project. But no matter how hard we tried, we couldn't get it scheduled. When we were on Oxford's campus, John was out of the country, and there were no other available opportunities before our deadline. It was a huge disappointment.

On our return trip home, our production team was standing in the Atlanta airport. You'd never guess who was standing five feet away: John Lennox! I couldn't believe it. I actually grabbed both of his arms and said, "John! It's Wes!" He smiled, and in his great Northern Irish accent, said, "Oh, my; this must be from the Lord!"

Clearly it was a divine appointment. He was headed to Seattle and invited us to join him on the trip. We had already been away for ten days and were eager to return home, but decided to take a quick trip to Seattle with him and return home the next day. As we

began working on the details, John said, "Or you could join me in
Florida. We'll be in Florida for two days before returning home."

I laughed. "Florida is much better," I said. "It's where we're
headed now. What city will you be in?"

He began flipping through a small appointment book and said,
"The house was a gift from a board member of Ravi Zacharias's
ministry in Cape Coral."

Cape Coral? That was my city!

"Are you kidding me? That's perfect." We arranged for the interview in Cape Coral, and John was able to speak directly with the
young guy whose story we had been following. So many intricate
details had had to come together for this conversation to happen.

When we acknowledge God's sovereignty over life and cultivate
an awareness of his presence, we discover that God appoints time
in ways that transcend our planning. God arranges connections to
bring about new life, whether it be salvation or a truckload of food.

Beth Guckenberger, executive director of Back2Back Ministries,
an international orphan care ministry, tells the story of a child at
one of their orphanages in Mexico who was told by the orphanage
director, "We don't have any food tonight, so we're going to pray
for God to give us our daily bread." The orphanage director asked
the child, "How do you want to pray?" The four-year-old boy said,
"I want to pray for steak, because when God brings dinner, he
brings steak." So they prayed for steak and waited.

Months earlier, while in the States, Beth had been contacted by
a businessman who said he was going to be in her area for a conference and would love to see the orphanages. She'd had no contact
with him since then—until that evening, when he called and said,
"I'm here, and if you can send over a truck, I've got a lot of supplies
to give the orphanage." Beth's husband, Todd, picked up the supplies while Beth called the orphanage director to tell him a delivery
truck was en route . . . with a trailer full of steaks. Neither Beth nor
the businessman knew of the boy's prayer.

When we respond to a God who is perfectly sovereign, immi-
nently present, and actively working in the world, stories like these
are what we get. God sends mathematicians to agnostics across

the world to share his gospel. God sends steaks to hungry kids in Mexican orphanages to feed them, body and soul. God answers prayers and permeates space. Such stories often emerge in tentative, unexpected, and fragile spaces that are easy to miss.

God will do what only God can do! Our part is living in a posture of receptivity, risking vulnerability, making room, adjusting course, and refusing to limit God to the artificial ceilings set by our own abilities, knowledge, expectations, and need for control.

So how do we cultivate the space in our own lives to respond to God's divine appointments? In the previous chapter we looked at the first three practices of radical hospitality contained in the letters of the acronym BREAD: begin with *xenia*, recruit mentors, and embrace tension. Two additional ways we can practice radical hospitality are to allow for margin and discern *kairos*.

Allow margin

There's no compassion without relationship, and there's no relationship without margin. Margin, according to Richard Swenson in his book by the same title, is "the space between ourselves and our limits. It's something held in reserve for contingencies or unanticipated situations."[1] Does that sound like a nonstarter as you think about your present commitments? It's helpful to distinguish margin from a vacuum. Not many of us sit around and wonder, "What am I going to do with all of this free time?" Fortunately, margin isn't limited to those who do. Margin can be viewed as an asterisk on an activity as much as the space for inactivity. The asterisk means that we are committed to holding that activity loosely and to not being surprised if it doesn't happen.

Here's what I mean. It doesn't matter what Mary was doing when the angel appeared. What mattered was her level of responsiveness. She was fully receptive: "I am the Lord's servant. . . . May your word to me be fulfilled" (Luke 1:38). Part of our work in building margin is placing a parenthetical asterisk next to our scheduled plans. As we strive to maintain an eternal perspective and remain fully present to God and people, we hold things loosely and allow God to redirect us when necessary.

Margin is squeezing in a little tighter to make room for someone we weren't expecting.

It's stopping in our tracks when a casual encounter with someone seems pregnant with opportunity. It's the expectation at the start of the day that somehow, somewhere, God is going to present an unexpected opportunity for an eternal impact.

Margin means remembering that some of our greatest opportunities in life can be prepared for but not planned. Drawing on agricultural imagery, we can prepare the soil, get rid of the weeds and toxins, and make the ground as fertile for growth as possible. But we also learn to recognize and trust God's role in the creation of life. The presence of margin in our lives is a sign that we recognize the distinction between our role and God's role.

To maintain such a posture through the course of a day, we need to cease a few habits: hurry, mental preoccupation, ambition, and a practical agnosticism. There are also a few habits we need to draw in, including regular meditation on God's Word, listening prayer, the keeping of Sabbath, and active listening to people.

Consider this news story from 2006. The Cougar Ace, a deep-sea transport ship, was en route from Asia to the United States with 4,812 Mazdas on board that were worth $117 million. On the night of July 24, the ship was about two hundred miles south of Alaska's Aleutian Islands and the crew began to prepare to enter U.S. waters. American maritime law requires that the ballast tanks, which fill with water to keep the ship steady, be emptied and refilled before entering U.S. waters in order to prevent contamination. Purge the old; make room for the new.

But this is tricky, because the two processes have to happen at the same time. If you purge the old water without simultaneously taking in the new, your ship immediately tips over. This is what happened to the Cougar Ace. It rolled onto its side and remained there for over a month. Every single one of the brand-new cars had to be destroyed.

In 1 Timothy 1:5, the apostle Paul writes that love "comes from a pure heart." His choice of words for "pure heart" is *catharsis cardia*, a "purging heart." A pure heart is one that is constantly drawing in what brings life and releasing what obstructs it.

We build margin in a similar way: we purge what hinders our receptivity to God's presence in our lives and draw in the habits that help cultivate it. We get rid of hurry and mental preoccupation because they make us fly past moments pregnant with opportunity and cause us to miss so much of life. We purge the natural tendency toward self-centeredness and reject ambition as a source of significance because both reflect a view of the world and humanity at odds with God's kingdom. A tower of Babel with a cross on top is still an idol.

As we purge the bad water, we simultaneously draw in the waters that bring life. We invite the Holy Spirit to be our counselor and guide. We allow God's Word to condition our expectations and shape our character. We pray, "Speak, for your servant is listening" (1 Samuel 3:10); "May your word to me be fulfilled" (Luke 1:38); and "Not my will, but yours" (Luke 22:42). And from this posture of receptivity, we respond in faith to the promptings we sense. The more we do, the more we learn to distinguish God's voice, the more our faith grows, and the more our stories change. There's a joy and even lightheartedness that comes when we seek to echo Jesus' words, "I do what I see the Father doing" (John 5:19, my paraphrase). We respond as best we can and trust God to work both through us and despite us. Allowing margin means creating and protecting the space for *kairos* moments, which we look at next.

Discern *kairos*

Two aspects of time converged when John Lennox and I met in the Atlanta airport. My team's flight to Fort Myers, Florida, was scheduled to depart at 8:43 p.m., and God had arranged for our meeting in that same space. The awareness of Immanuel (God with us) changes our perception of time. We live within chronological time as well as within God's appointed time. Our view of the world and time are simply porous to God's presence with us. The Greeks had two words for these two concepts of time: *chronos* (chronological time) and *kairos* (appointed time).

Kairos moments are always divine appointments, but they are not always at convenient times. John Lennox was a welcomed surprise, and it was easy to adjust course to make room for the interruption; however, most of my *kairos* moments are of a different sort. In the story of the good Samaritan, it's easy to vilify the religious leaders who walked past an injured man in a ditch without helping. They clearly missed a *kairos* moment. The story is a parable, but it's easy to imagine it was based on a true story. Those religious leaders didn't know the story would be forever chronicled in human history! I pass people in need every day, and if I knew Jesus was going to tell the story for the world to learn from, I'd be more careful.

But you can't stop for every person in need or you won't get anywhere, right? Jesus himself didn't help everyone in need.

Embracing inconvenience is a two-part mind-set shift. The first part is recognizing inconveniences as potential divine appointments. The second part is discerning which ones to respond to. The first part is harder than it sounds.

Last night, I chose an inferior burger establishment simply because it had a drive-through. How sad is that? There is a local burger restaurant that gets rave reviews. But I chose the chain restaurant because I could get in and out of there in less than five minutes. I find it infinitely easier to extol the virtue of embracing inconvenience as the space for unexpected divine appointments than I do to actually embrace it in the middle of the day.

Two nights ago, as I got off the train I take to go into the city for grad school classes, a guy fell in the street right in front of me and started having a seizure. His body was convulsing and foam was streaming out of his mouth. Without a second thought, I dropped my bag, rolled him onto his side, and gently held his head so it wouldn't keep smacking against the pavement. A woman called 911, and within five minutes the paramedics were there to take over.

The call to respond was unmistakable and directly in my face. But I cannot tell you how many times I encounter less sensational and slightly less direct opportunities with strangers in which I silently hope to avoid an obligatory connection with them. *Oh, please don't talk to me,* I think to myself. *It's just a bad time.* This is especially true if the need is common and one that I encounter frequently. One homeless family? I'm glad to help. Thirty homeless individuals in a two-block area? I'd prefer to walk by without being noticed.

Inconvenience says, "Excuse me, I need to interrupt your regularly scheduled life to bring you something you didn't see coming." Our defenses naturally rise up and we scour our mental Rolodexes for the most efficient, appropriate, and uncallous way to cut it off at the pass. "No, I'm sorry . . ." "I'd love to, but . . ."

Maybe receptivity to inconvenience comes more naturally for you, but it's something I've had to work really hard at. Inconvenience often opens doors to hospitality in the same way that hospitality opens doors to compassion, but we have to be deliberately paying attention. Practically, discerning *kairos* requires that my attention shifts from myopic expectation and desire for how the day will unfold, to an expectant attention to others.

The word *inconvenient* literally means "not fitting." For many in the West, the reasons that so many events and people are "not fitting" into our lives include a frenetic pace, mental preoccupation, fear, self-centeredness, and really good earbuds that cancel out the entire world. And yet the "not fitting" encounters often get the ball rolling to tremendous breakthroughs and life-giving encounters with people.

Saint Francis of Assisi once spoke of an encounter with a man in need whom he was tempted to ignore. Upon later reflection, Saint Francis felt as if the man had been an angel. From that day forward, he chose to follow Hebrews 13:2 and treat every stranger as an angel. The idea of *theoxeny* (divine + hospitality) that we looked at in chapter 7 can help us with the first part of this mind-set shift. Every person is an image-bearer of God, and an encounter that may first appear as an ill-timed inconvenience may be a part of God's plan.

The more difficult question is discerning which inconveniences to embrace. From the posture we've been describing, the task of discerning potential *kairos* moments is a largely intuitive one. Now, that doesn't mean we need to wait for a special prompting from the Lord to respond graciously to unexpected opportunities. Scripture offers us ample justification to walk an extra mile for someone, open our doors to strangers, and generally use our time and resources to bless people. If a small detour or act of kindness has the potential to bless someone and you're able to do it without great cost, don't hesitate to do it. Not everything we do needs to be perfectly scalable or even make perfect sense. So many of the encounters that I later viewed as divine appointments fall into this category. I didn't see the potential ahead of time or sense a strong prompting from the Lord. The opportunity appeared like a slight opening, with faint rays of light peering through.

Where there's a cost to such an act, and you're unsure whether you should respond, it's better to err on the side of saying yes than no. Ask the Lord for brakes rather than an engine. In the case of thirty homeless people on a single block and the feeling of being overwhelmed by the need, know that it's perfectly okay to extend radical hospitality to one. At the pool of Bethesda, in John 5, Jesus approached a single guy and asked the question, "Do you want to get well?" If you pass the same group often, that's a different matter altogether than an unexpected *kairos* moment. Come up with a plan to walk as the favor of God among them. Learn names, grab an extra slice of pizza, and share a meal. Eventually, in addition to embodying a healing presence and extending radical hospitality, find ways to address the deeper issues, which we'll look at in part 3 of this book.

The specifics will work their way out once our perspective and posture are rightly aligned. In the same way that an all-compelling *why* eventually finds the appropriate *how*, the posture of radical hospitality will find ways to embrace inconveniences with wisdom and grace.

By building in margin and embracing inconveniences, we are more poised to respond to God's *kairos* moments. The more we do these things, the more our stories won't make sense apart from God's work in our lives.

Turning radical hospitality into a way of life

Radical hospitality is one of the greatest gifts we can give our communities. We need individuals and families willing to move food pantries into their kitchens, put people first, risk vulnerability, leave space, and anticipate *kairos* moments with eager expectancy. It's a countercultural way to live, but it's also part of the basic package of following Jesus. We extend hospitality to strangers, heal the sick, and care for the marginalized. As we do, we will see new life rise up all around us.

The five practices of radical hospitality (begin with *xenia*, recruit mentors, embrace tension, allow margin, and discern *kairos*) help us see and respond to the opportunities God presents to us daily.

For followers of Jesus, an eternal worldview helps bring clarity to the practical questions about radical hospitality. When we shift our mind-set from the temporal to the eternal, our priorities shift with it.

If God is sovereign, present, and actively at work in this world, redeeming his creation; if people are eternal beings with whom God longs to reconcile himself; and if we join God in his ministry of reconciliation, then eternity-changing opportunities are always before us! Our posture of being fully present to God and people opens the door to these opportunities for new life to flourish.

Every day we can say, as Mary said to the angel who brought the unexpected pronouncement of Jesus' coming: "I am the Lord's servant. . . . May your word to me be fulfilled" (Luke 1:38). Such encounters are never on the schedule. But the schedule—like the budget and the future plans—are all held loosely. We expect God to arrange divine appointments and cross our path with unexpected opportunities for new life. May it be so!

HEALING PRESENCE

RADICAL HOSPITALITY

COLLECTIVE EMPOWERMENT

Part III

Collective Empowerment: Open the Right Doors

10

A City of Refuge

In the Negev Desert in southern Israel, an area once thought to be uninhabitable, farmers are busy exporting food and water. Despite rapid growth and a population density more than six times what the desert was thought to be able to support, Israel's desert has become Europe's primary source of winter vegetables.

After centuries of overgrazing and deforestation, the southern desert in Israel, which occupies 60 percent of the country's total land, has become a model for how deserts can bloom. Despite the fact that Israel is one of the driest countries in the world, it is the only country in the world where the desert is receding. How did this happen?

Seth Siegel, in his book, *Let There Be Water: Israel's Solution for a Water-Starved World*, highlights a few of Israel's breakthroughs that can be applied elsewhere.[1] Two of the biggest breakthroughs help shed light on how communities flourish.

Israel has pioneered some of the most advanced agricultural technologies in the last hundred years, including use of filtration devices, desalinization techniques, and drip irrigation. Drip irrigation, in which small pipes with tiny holes deliver the right amount of water and nutrients to the roots of the plants, has been especially important in allowing deserts to become gardens.

Drip irrigation is a contrast to the most common and age-old method of flood irrigation, in which an entire field is covered with water to ensure the roots receive the nutrients needed for growth. But more than 60 percent of the water is lost in the process. Israel couldn't afford such waste. So the people worked tirelessly to discover exactly what was needed for life to thrive in the desert and then experimented to find the most efficient delivery systems to get it there. They experimented, measured, and adapted until they could deliver the right amount of the right resource to the right place. This careful attention to detail; decisive, bold, and long-range vision; and continual adaptation of methods to achieve the needed end provides a model for how deserts can bloom.

Israel's second major breakthrough that holds application for communities is the sheer lack of waste. Some 85 percent of sewage in Israel is recycled. In the United States, water that flows out of our homes undergoes a significant and expensive treatment process and is then released into nearby bodies of water. In other words: we process the water until it is nearly drinkable—and then we discard it. Israel created a delivery system to recycle this water for agricultural purposes. The result has been a sustainable surplus that is feeding millions and millions of people.

Israel found limited amounts of brackish water when people went drilling. So the citizens worked tirelessly on cost-effective desalinization and filtration systems and learned how to use the brackish water for agriculture. Now you can visit a fish farm in the middle of the desert where barramundi, an edible fish that thrives in brackish water, are being raised in an olive orchard, because olive trees also thrive on the salty water.

Due to necessity and a lack of resources, Israel had to study its environment, learn what works, pioneer technologies to expand and deliver precious resources, and pay careful attention to detail in its continual adaptation of methods to produce fruitful crops in harsh conditions. Today, leaders from other countries are touring fields and desalinization plants in the middle of a desert to learn how they bloom.

Think about the potential impact if a similar level of rigor and verve were applied to the large-scale challenges in our communities. What could we learn from such an approach for our pursuit of community flourishing? Let's start with a consideration of frameworks.

What is collective empowerment?
Collective empowerment is the work of establishing rightly placed doors and nets, primarily by those who will access them. People need safe places to land and opportunities and empowerment to flourish. We need to resist all forms of aid that perpetuate cycles of dependency, and to learn to recognize the unintentional decisions responsible for it. A key aspect of collective empowerment is involving potential recipients of services in the early work of determining what's needed, why, and how it should happen. Empowerment necessitates ownership. Paulo Freire, in *The Pedagogy of the Oppressed*, writes, "One cannot expect positive results from a program which fails to respect the particular view of the world held by the people. Such a program constitutes cultural invasion, good intentions notwithstanding."[2]

Like those who pursued water in Israel's desert, we will need to understand our geography well, build a team of local stakeholders who are personally involved in all stages of the work, have a compelling vision to orient our work, develop strategies to realize it, measure progress, and adapt where necessary.

Let's use child poverty as an example for how these principles could translate into an effective framework for the work of collective empowerment.

Say you gather a group of us to pray and fast for our community. This group is almost all community members, including those experiencing needs we expect to address and stakeholders in health, education, government, social services, nonprofit, and the church. We go out on prayer walks in neighborhoods and ask God to unveil our eyes to see what God sees. Building on the principle of healing presence, we immerse ourselves in the posture of loving, listening, discerning, and responding. Embodying radical hospitality, we invite neighbors and neighbor kids into our homes for conversation and fellowship. We extend ourselves and open our homes to those around us.

As we move into the stage of collective empowerment, we begin to gather broader data on our community. We draw quantitative data from online sources and local community assessments. We also listen to neighbors and invite them to join us in the very beginning. Through these conversations and the use of surveys, listening sessions, interviews, and direct observation, we identify key strengths and opportunities in the community. One area that continues to rise to the surface is opportunities for children from low-income households. It's where we most "sense the heat" to draw in closer. So we decide to draw a circle around the children in our community and say, "Every child in this community will have the opportunity to know their God-given identity and realize their God-given potential."

On the basis of what we learn, we identify five key outcomes for our collective empowerment strategy:

1. *Expand knowledge.* We will gather and distribute relevant, trustworthy, and accessible information on the current needs, opportunities, and progress of our kids in the community.
2. *Early childhood education.* We will establish high-quality preschool and childcare for low-income families.
3. *Parenting education and support.* We will organize proactive and responsive support among neighbors with an emphasis on new parents, single parents, and low-income families.
4. *Foster care.* We will ensure that every child has a loving family and every adoptable child finds a forever home.
5. *School mentoring.* We will work with every school in the area to establish a relational support network.

We are well aware of our many uncertainties, insecurities, and deficits, but we have a Henri Dunant–like verve to startle our collective conscience: "Our kids need us to do better!" We match a bold and lofty vision with a rigorous and highly detailed pursuit of the best ways to realize it. We surround ourselves with leaders who are ahead of us, work collaboratively with others engaged in similar work, and become good students of best practices. We constantly and passionately tell a different and more compelling narrative about our kids. And with clear and measurable goals in place, we begin the aligning and developing work to see that story come to life.

We start our work with two initiatives that can generate further momentum and some short-term wins: to expand knowledge and support foster and adoption initiatives. There are already strengths in these areas to build on, and they hold the most resonance within our group. The clear vision and broad-based empowerment of community members allows us to set up an open-source platform for others to join in the work in many ways, directly and indirectly.

In this example, the framework is based on several key values and related strategies: collective ownership, knowledge of a defined geography, a clear vision that rises from prayer and research, an open-source approach to building the bridges necessary to realize it, and measurements that provide feedback loops to adjust initiatives where necessary.

To simplify the framework, let's use the acronym DOOR to describe the four key practices of collective empowerment:

- Define a geography and know it
- Observe what works and implement it
- Operate with measurements and adapt where necessary
- Radiate the vision and empower others

The work of collective empowerment can feel overwhelming and appear impossible when we compare our present situation and the future we imagine. Before we jump in, let me share two encouraging stories that can help demystify how busy and flawed individuals become catalysts for large-scale and deeply needed change in our communities.

Catalysts for change

I recently had a meeting with a few colleagues at a restaurant, and our server was a middle-aged woman in long-term recovery. She was homeless five years ago, although you would never guess her past. After her shift ended, she was headed to the capitol to testify at a hearing on the opioid epidemic in Pennsylvania. Like Robin, this woman now extends radical hospitality to other women pursuing recovery and is working on multiple levels to empower them to step forward into the fullness of life God offers.

I only know her story because someone in our group helped her get into treatment. When we walked into the restaurant and they saw each other, there was an immediate and soulful embrace. The server grabbed her arm: "*This* woman! I wouldn't be alive today without her." Our friend downplayed it. "I just invited her into the detox center. She did the work."

Our colleague had turned an abandoned home into a detox center. She had no money and just a couple of friends in recovery willing to help. That center has recently spread to three recovery centers and has expanded services. Their services blend Christian discipleship and evidence-based practices, and 90 percent of their referrals come from the court system. Both of these women know the numbers, the risks, and the resources. They're spending themselves well to see new life rise up from the desert. What started with a healing presence and radical hospitality is now expanding with these practices of collective empowerment. Women needed help with job training, so a program was established that preserved the posture of compassion while providing employment assistance. The structured forms of support were a logical extension of the relational connections.

Here's another inspiring story of collective empowerment. In Singapore, a young mother came across a statistic that she wasn't able to get out of her mind: the number of foster children living in group homes. Within a few miles of her family's home, there were 362 children in foster care and 804 children in institutionalized care. As a new mom, her heart broke for these kids.

She began to pray for these children, ask social workers and government officials why there were so many children in institutionalized care and how the system worked, and visit the orphanages. She wasn't raised in foster care and doesn't have a shared experience to draw her into it. She just has a deep sense that this isn't how it's supposed to be. Her plate is completely full, and she doesn't see herself as a leader. There's nothing in her background to suggest she's the one to help orphaned children in Singapore. But she has prayed, gathered the data, and come to believe, in her words: "Something has to be done!" She possesses a Henri Dunant–like verve to jump in—despite all the reasons not to. She possesses the rigor to do whatever is necessary for these kids to find a good home.

Right now, the small community group she formed is working tirelessly to find good homes for those 804 children. For her small group, the bridge to collective empowerment was the sheer disconnect between the reality and the kingdom as they prayed, "Jesus, your kingdom here, as it is in heaven."

Cities of refuge in ancient Israel

In the Old Testament, six cities in Israel were set apart as "cities of refuge" (see Joshua 20; Numbers 35:9-15). These asylum cities were defined areas where the normal laws of retribution were suspended. If someone unintentionally killed another person, he or she could flee to one of these cities and receive protection and care. There were three of these cities on each side of the Jordan River, and they were places of worship and were open to all people, not just the people of Israel.

The image of a city of refuge has long captivated me: a defined geographic space where the normal ways of society are turned upside down, and where the places most known for worship extend a healing presence to those who need it.

Creating a city of refuge—a safe place to land for people regardless of their background or beliefs—requires a collective healing presence in a community. Our opportunities as individuals and families are immense, but there is something really special when a community develops a reputation for being a place of healing and restoration—a place about which people can say, "If I can just get there, I can start to put the pieces back together."

Michelle, one of the women Robin has mentored in the recovery community, was trafficked for over ten years. After one relapse, Michelle said to Robin, "I know I can do life again. I just need some help right now." She's finding it in a small church that has fully embraced the ministry of addiction recovery. She has told a couple of friends, "When a bed opens here, you need to grab it." When a church establishes a collective healing presence in its community and gains a reputation as a place where dead things come to life, it will never need to worry about whether its voice will be heard.

A young Somali friend of mine escaped his hometown with his mother and eight siblings. His father had been brutally murdered in their home, right before their eyes. They fled to the largest refugee camp in the world, the Dadaab camp in Kenya, where they met an elderly Mennonite missionary couple who taught the children English and basic computer programming. In 2014, the family was able to move to Pennsylvania, and they were welcomed by a family who helped them with every detail of their resettlement. This family and their small group invited the refugees to backyard picnics, taught the mother how to drive, and helped her secure a driver's license, helped her register for certified nursing assistant classes, signed the kids up for their new schools, and assisted with many other details. The family had responded to a request from their church, which was collaborating with other churches and nonprofits to establish a city of refuge for these refugees. This family would be the first to say that the blessing is theirs: the Somali family is an inspiration and gift to their community. In 2016, just a year and a half after their arrival, the Somali family is instrumental in welcoming new families and coordinating support networks.

In October 2016, my Somali friend was invited to the White House to speak about the refugee crisis and how we should respond. He spoke in perfect English about the need to make room for those displaced, because their presence is a gift rather than a burden. The retired Mennonite couple who first taught his family English would have enjoyed hearing his tribute to "those who showed me a way of peace."

What would a city of refuge look like in your community? Building on the posture of compassion with healing presence and radical hospitality, a great beginning toward collective empowerment is simply a full immersion in our communities using four key practices. The first—defining a geography and knowing it inside and out—is best undertaken with prayer and fasting. "God, may your kingdom come here as it is in heaven," we pray. "Unveil our eyes to see what you see and how we can collaborate with your redemptive work in this community."

That's our next step: defining a geography and knowing it. And the good news is that it's never been easier.

11

Draw the Circle

"Our historic aim will be for ours to be the first generation to end child poverty." In March 1999, Tony Blair, then prime minister of the United Kingdom, made this pledge. The country's child poverty rate had been rising and was nearly 20 percent at the time of the announcement. Although Blair had no clear plan at the beginning, in eight years, Britain managed to cut the child poverty rate in half! During this time (1999–2007), the child poverty rate in the United States continued to climb. Jane Waldfogel, in her book *Britain's War on Poverty* and in other writings and lectures, evaluates the British strategy and expounds on the lessons others can learn from it.[1] Regardless of the specific steps, however, one thing is clear: there's a power in drawing a circle and proclaiming, "It's going to be different in here!"

Part of that power is simply acknowledging the environmental factors for health and disease. Like with a patient with a contagious disease in a contaminated hospital who's eating food that exacerbates his illness, addressing any one of the issues to the exclusion of the others is better than nothing, but it's unlikely to heal the patient. Disjointed or half-measured approaches may show signs of success, but they won't yield real change in the long term. Healing, in this case, requires looking both at the hospital and inside the cells.

Our social context exerts so many intangible and imperceptible influences on our lives that intentionality alone is unable to fully counteract them. Like real estate, health has a whole lot to do with location. When we realize how much context affects individuals, we take the first step toward collective empowerment.

Define a geography and know it

Real change in our communities requires that we define a geography and know it well. Real change and movement toward collective empowerment requires what is called a "systems perspective," which can be illuminated through community mapping. Let's look at these two concepts in more detail.

Adopt a systems perspective

Tobler's first law of geography states, "Everything is related to everything else, but near things are more related than distant things." Family systems yield greater influence than neighborhood characteristics. And neighborhood characteristics yield greater influence than the group meeting across town that happens once a week. Because of the porous nature of our lives, a geographic circle is preferable to an isolated project that lacks a view of the environmental factors affecting the work.

Learning to view the world from a systems perspective means paying attention to the ways that individual behaviors and realities are connected to larger systems and networks. Becoming a good student of a community's risk and protective factors is a bit like basic detective work. We can gather all kinds of data on our community, but how do we best make sense of it? The dots need to connect into a coherent story. How does the data square with the stories people are telling about their primary challenges and opportunities? What is the relationship between household dynamics and economic factors? A systems approach within a clearly defined geography allows you to work simultaneously on macro, mezzo, and micro levels.

The work of community flourishing is infinitely more complex than drawing sustainable and fresh water out of a desert. But our takeaway from that example could be that we have to work all that much harder to learn and adapt rather than settle for an indiscriminate allocation of resources and anecdotal measurements.

The needs and opportunities in our communities are simply too great to settle for the equivalent of flood irrigation techniques. A "more is better" approach to our community's flourishing—that is, an indiscriminate allocation of resources and anecdotal measurements—needs to be permanently set aside. "More is better" is not smart compassion. We need a more careful and deliberate pursuit of real change. We need imagination to see a different and better vision, the verve to draw the circle and name it, and the rigor to pursue it. We need steely resolve, collaboration, patience, a long-term view, courage, and the sheer confidence that our community can and will flourish.

Map your community

Here's a short quiz. How well do you know the census tract where you live?

1. How many households live below the poverty line?
2. How many households are led by single parents?
3. Do college graduates outnumber the individuals who obtained less than a twelfth-grade education?
4. How many children live in homes without a biological parent?
5. How many children in foster care are available for adoption?

If you're like many people, you have a rough idea of the answers for your immediate neighborhood but you're unsure of the boundary lines for your census tract. The good news is that you can know the answers to these questions with a quick search of federal and community development websites. A quick search of online databases can reveal the number of reports of human trafficking in your area, as well as how your area compares to state and national averages on issues such as teen births, sexually transmitted diseases, overdose deaths, access to primary and mental healthcare, graduation rates, children in poverty, single parents, crime indexes, housing problems, and much more.

When it comes to defining a geography, the U.S. Census Bureau provides a helpful classification system for distinguishing neighborhoods in the United States. Counties and zip codes may be sufficient for drawing boundaries, but the Census Bureau provides smaller levels of classification, including census tracts and blocks. Census tracts are county subdivisions that comprise a population between 1,200 and 8,000, and optimally around 4,000 people. They are organized as relatively permanent neighborhoods, emphasize homogeneity with respect to population characteristics, economic status, and living conditions, and vary in size depending on population density. Census blocks are the smallest and most basic building block for all geographic boundaries. In a city, a census block looks like a city block bounded by streets on all sides. In areas that are less dense, the block will be larger. To give some perspective, there are 3,143 counties in the United States; in the 2010 census, there were 74,134 census tracts and 11,078,297 census blocks.

While the U.S. census is only conducted every ten years, the Census Bureau's American Community Survey (ACS) is a statistical survey that gathers socioeconomic, housing, and demographic information on three and a half million households every year. Together, the census and ACS provide a basic starting point for defining and knowing a geography, and their data is easily accessible online.

You can use a mapping program like Google Earth and the census classification system to get started. Programs like Google Earth allow you to draw boundary lines and even upload spreadsheets with information, such as addresses. Once you've defined an area of focus, you can supplement census and ACS data with local needs and asset assessments, which can often be obtained through community foundations, local hospitals, or housing authorities. Data is becoming increasingly available, and a little detective work can go a long way. You may be surprised (and a little concerned) at how much you can access online. You will also find helpful guidance from people with firsthand knowledge of the topic. If you're interested in learning more about community mapping, you can find helpful resources and services at the City of Refuge website, refuge.life.

Observe what works and implement it

Once you've defined a geography and taken a good look at the needs and resources in your local area, the work of collective empowerment turns to observing what works and implementing it. An important aspect of observing a community is looking at its positive attributes, not just its deficits. It's very tempting to look at a community and diagnose all that is wrong with it. But what if we were to reverse that approach and seek out the good that is there? What if we first looked not at the weaknesses, but the strengths?

Work from a strengths-based approach

The shift to a strengths-based approach in our work with communities is seldom instinctive, but when it's implemented, it always yields surprising results. Let's use gun violence as an example. If you were tasked with curbing gun violence in metro areas in the United States, how would you go about it?

In the United States, an epidemiologist named Gary Slutkin began to look at gun violence from a public health perspective. He found that the spread of violence followed patterns similar to the spread of infectious diseases he had battled for ten years in Africa. "Social epidemiology" took epidemiological principles of intervention and applied them to gun violence. You can predict patterns, identify "hosts," send in "interrupters," and engage in the same painstaking, person-by-person intervention necessary to stop the spread of a disease.[2]

Slutkin first tested his model in West Garfield, the most violent community in Chicago at the time, and found remarkable success. The state of Illinois then expanded the program to fifteen communities and increased the number of interrupters from twenty to eighty. That year, homicides declined in Chicago by 25 percent. Slogans like "Don't shoot. I want to grow up" and hospital-based violence prevention programs were part of a holistic and highly relational strategy to get to the root of violence.

Cure Violence, the nonprofit that grew out of Slutkin's research, works from a strengths-based perspective. The key to this violence-prevention work is the interrupter: a person with credibility who is known and respected in the community and who is able to help a potential aggressor chart an alternative path. Within the Core Violence model, interrupters build rapport with those likely to perpetuate a violent act, and they walk with them step-by-step down an alternative path. They listen, empathize, and advocate. This relationship built on trust is the key catalyst for stopping the spread of violence. A documentary called *The Interrupters* tells the story of three of these individuals and how they use their own experiences with street violence to help cure violence in their Chicago community. Identifying community assets like interrupters happens when you work out of a strengths-based perspective. If you are only looking for wounds that need to be healed, you might miss out on the very people who can be instrumental in the healing.

Make connections between things that already belong together

Cure Violence is a good example of how a systems perspective can help make sense of large and complex social problems. The principles of epidemiology—find patterns, identify hosts, send in interrupters to stop the spread of disease—are broadly applicable to our work in invigorating life change in our communities. Sometimes the greatest gift of the church to the collective empowerment of a community is identifying and strengthening connections between individuals and nonprofits already at work. Collective empowerment doesn't always mean building something new; sometimes it means simply strengthening connections that are already there.

Within the Cure Violence model, interrupters are people who come with immediate credibility because of their own history. They are already living and working within the community; they just need to be connected to young people at risk for crime and to one another.

Interrupters also push for reform. Those who advocate the Cure Violence model are not content to treat symptoms of violence or to work exclusively on a reactionary and individualistic level. They work from a systems and strengths-based perspective. If you're an interrupter on a given block, you're concerned and engaged with all factors that contribute to the flourishing and *dis*ease of the individuals and families on that block. You're making and naming connections.

The idea of building on strengths and making connections takes on an even deeper meaning when viewed in light of God's work around us. God is at work in ways far beyond us. He is sovereign over every aspect of life. When we open and even knock down doors for others in response to where we see God at work, we can rest in the knowledge that "God's work done God's way will never lack God's supply." Hudson Taylor discovered this great truth when he responded in faithful obedience to God's call to empty himself for others. It is a truth we will discover in our own way when our work flows from a place of intimacy with God rather than from human wisdom alone.

These first two parts of the DOOR collective empowerment strategy—define a geography and know it, and observe what works and implement it—draw us into the core work of collective empowerment that is most likely to yield real change. First, when we define a geography, there's sheer power in drawing the circle, expecting change, and looking simultaneously at the macro, mezzo, and micro level. Second, when we observe what works and implement it, we respond to where God is already at work and we learn from the wisdom of best practices. This means operating from a strengths-based perspective and empowering local ownership.

If your group or congregation pursues these first two aspects of collective empowerment, you are well aligned to see real changes emerge.

Let's take a look at a few inspiring examples of improbable change—examples from history that show ways women and men have put collective empowerment into practice.

Three lessons from history
Pittsburgh, 1848
Cholera, a deadly and contagious disease, is spreading across the city at an alarming rate. Lutheran pastor William Passavant is walking the streets one afternoon and senses a vision from the Lord: "This city needs a hospital." This is an easy vision to dismiss when you have no money, medical education, experience, or

connections. Never mind: in this case, God has spoken. The circle has been drawn. So Passavant sets out to build a hospital.

He saves as much money as he can for a down payment on the "hospital," which is nothing more than a small house with a few beds. He borrows an old stove, a few beds, and some chairs. His first patients are sick and wounded soldiers returning home from the Mexican-American War. He learns everything he can about hospital management and invites Christians with medical knowledge to help him build the hospital and care for patients.

When the word spreads around the neighborhood that Passavant is taking in cholera patients, the neighbors go ballistic and stage protests and throw rocks at the house. The mayor eventually intervenes and gives Passavant an ultimatum: remove the cholera patients or vacate the building.

Picture this scene: With little money and no idea where they will land, Passavant, his staff, and the patients start walking to find another home. Patients too sick to walk are placed in their beds and pushed on carts. They're praying and singing as they walk. Passavant finds an empty building that was once a girls' school and gets permission to temporarily house the patients there.

Today, that hospital is University of Pittsburgh Medical Center Passavant, the largest private employer in Pennsylvania, with more than sixty-two thousand employees operating more than twenty academic, community, and specialty hospitals and four hundred outpatient sites.

Like Henri Dunant of the Red Cross, Passavant saw a vision of new life: "There must be a hospital!" It wasn't a question or a suggestion. It also didn't matter that there was no money or place. There *must* be a hospital. For Passavant and Dunant, the world was mutable. Things could change. And not just small things.

For Passavant, the development of future hospitals, orphanages, and schools would each have their own version of the same story: big vision, excruciatingly small beginning, massive resistance, refusal to retreat, and, finally, the resistance yields to unexpected breakthrough and provision. Like the emergence of water in deserts, it's easy to see the outcomes and miss the tireless and persistent work on intricate details and continual adaptation of methods to realize a much-needed but very fragile vision.

London, 1854

The first metropolitan experiment in the world isn't going well. Victorian London, with its nearly two and a half million people within a thirty-mile perimeter, is the world's largest, densest, and most putrid city ever built. London is resting on an archaic and hemorrhaging public infrastructure, and on lethal ideas about health and disease. In the Soho District, families keep cesspools in their basement and livestock in their homes. If you ask people, "What's the cause of rampant disease?" their clear answer is, "Bad air."

Cholera is spreading across Britain as well. The disease is terrorizing the public consciousness. To address the crisis, Parliament in 1846 passes the Nuisance Removal and Diseases Prevention Act, which encourages families to clean their homes and dump their waste in the River Thames. "Bad air" is the problem, and one way or another, their main water source needs to double as their collective sewer. Officers with the London Metropolitan Sewers Commission travel around the city instructing all homes to empty their cesspools and sewage pits into the river.

Between August 31 and September 2, 1854, 127 people in Soho suddenly die from cholera in what will become the worst outbreak the city has ever seen. As people evacuate the area, a local doctor goes to the heart of the outbreak. John Snow, who will later become known as the father of epidemiology, studied cholera in his apprenticeship in New Castle, and he believes the disease is ingested rather than inhaled. For years he has studied the disease under the microscope and in the newspaper, following its path through death reports. He enlists the help of a local priest, Henry Whitehead, a well-known and trusted community leader. Together, they interview people and eventually trace the source of the outbreak to the popular water pump at 40 Broad Street, which draws from a well beneath the Golden Square, home to some of the poorest and most overcrowded neighborhoods in London.

From their interviews, they construct a map of the cholera-related fatalities. This map offers a different way of seeing cholera. The deaths have a clear epicenter. They have a point of origin. It isn't a matter of "bad air"; it is a matter of contaminated water. Snow and Whitehead's map eventually changes perceptions of the disease, and later specific policies, so that by the next major cholera outbreak, which will be the last, people are instructed to boil water.

Chicago, 1889

Like London, Chicago is quickly becoming a modern metropolitan city. In two generations, massive immigration will help the population of Chicago swell from five hundred thousand to nearly three million. The rapid and crowded growth brings with it widespread disease, poverty, and a high infant mortality rate. Anyone with resources is fleeing the city—except a group of women, led by Jane Addams, who run right into the heart of it. Like a truck of storm-chasers barreling down an empty highway toward a hurricane after a mass evacuation, these women go directly against the tide of the upper-middle-class response to the changes in their city.

Imagine this is your community. Everyone is listing their home, trying to get out as much value as they can. Parents are worried about their children's safety and education. In the middle of the frenzy to get out, what would you say if a friend offered a different interpretation: "Everyone is going in the wrong direction. We need to get in there. What do you say?"

Jane and a couple of friends move into the Hull House, strategically located in downtown Chicago, with a vision to help the city flourish. They begin their work by moving from building to building with a detailed questionnaire. They ask residents, "What country are you from? Where do you work? How much do you make?" In 1895 they publish *The Hull-House Maps and Papers*, which dispels myths, exposes real needs, and launches campaigns. Ultimately, through their mapping work, the women of Hull House save many tens of thousands of lives by lowering infant and maternal mortality rates and helping with food, medical care, work, and educational issues. Their work sets off a ripple effect that simply cannot be measured.

Rather than rest on assumptions of what was needed and what was possible, Jane Addams and her coworkers sought empirical data to guide their strategies. "I think we should . . ." wasn't good enough to initiate a project. Heartwarming anecdotes were nice, but they weren't a measure of success. The women of Hull House were after real change. So instead of handing out bread and medicine alone, they identified and engaged the core sources of vitality and *dis*ease.

Where wisdom and heart meet

Addams's work in Chicago, Passavant's work in Pittsburgh, and Snow and Whitehead's work in London: these efforts reveal a few consistent themes that contributed to their breakthroughs. For one, they defined a geography and got to know it well. Second, they figured out what was working and they implemented it.

Ultimately, they pressed through adversity with an indomitable and optimistic spirit.

A Hull House–sized vision without people willing to embody it wouldn't have generated the same results. Their vision permeated their marrow and moved their feet. It's also true that people with the same level of dedication but devoid of the vision and strategy wouldn't have generated the same results. The same is true for Snow and Whitehead's work in London. Heart and strategy must coalesce and reinforce each other.

Today, there are many examples of these principles of collective empowerment at work. In 1997, Becca Stevens opened a house and invited five prostitutes to live with her. Today, Thistle Farms has provided more than seven hundred women, at no cost to them, two full years of housing, food, therapy, medical care, dental care, education, and job training. On average, these women were first sexually abused between the ages of seven and eleven, have been arrested a hundred times, and have spent twelve years in prostitution. In addition to the residential program, which has an 85 percent successful completion rate, Thistle Farms runs a flourishing social enterprise and education and outreach initiative to support an ever-growing "community of survivors that believes love heals." It started in a single home with healing presence and radical hospitality. It then expanded its reach to empower thousands of women through its advocacy, education, and social enterprise work.

Karen Olson was rushing to a meeting one afternoon when she passed a homeless woman. She bought her a sandwich and listened to her story. With her young sons, she began delivering lunches to homeless people and learning as much as she could about how to help them secure housing. A small group of churches began opening their buildings at night, and the YMCA provided showers and a family daycare center. A car dealership discounted a van. Over time, this small group of churches grew into a national network. Today, Family Promise is helping lead a national movement to end homelessness and provide housing first.

In the fall of 2008, the first Wait No More event was held at New Life Church in Colorado Springs to highlight the opportunities to adopt children through the foster care system. Dr. Sharon Ford had spent more than twenty years advocating for kids in foster care, and hoped the event would lead a few dozen families to start the adoption process for a waiting child or sibling group. Instead, more than 265 families responded to the invitation and started the process of adopting through foster care. By early 2016, Wait No More events had been held in twenty states, with more than 3,200 families initiating the process of adopting through foster care.

Like John Perkins in Mississippi and Luis Cortes in Philadelphia, these individuals started with the posture of compassion: proximity, solidarity, and emotional connectedness. Their ministry was *with* people, not just *to* or *for* them. As their healing presence and radical hospitality expanded into collective empowerment, the structured forms of support remained a logical extension of the relational connections.

But to what end?

It's an important question for the pursuit of collective empowerment. What's the problem we're trying to solve and what does success look like? A clear vision and carefully constructed strategy paves the way for the third principle of the DOOR collective empowerment framework: operate with measurements and adapt where necessary.

12

To What End?

True north is not an intuitive reality for people. A surprising aspect of human nature is that we cannot move forward in a straight line without a fixed point of reference. Our internal gyroscopes are simply off.

Imagine that you are blindfolded and led into a wide-open field. A hundred yards away and directly across from you sits a table with $1 million stacked on it. If you were told, "The money is yours if you walk directly to it without turning around," there's about a zero percent chance you'd reach it. No one is sure why, but for some reason, we naturally walk in circles. The experiment (albeit without $1 million) has been done multiple times in many countries, with people walking, driving, or swimming blindfolded, or simply in foggy weather. It's the same result every time. The person starts out straight, but then makes a slight turn. That turn increases in degree until the person is walking in circles. The circles grow tighter the longer the person moves forward. Without a fixed point of reference, we cannot walk straight.

In our work of collective empowerment—stewarding life on a community level—we simply cannot trust our instincts alone. Revelation from God helps us draw the circle and set the course, but Scripture clearly supports the mutual embrace of revelation and wisdom gained through experience. Before we look too closely at the role of measurements, we need to make a distinction about the appropriate use of data for decision making.

Operate with measurements and adapt where necessary

We need data-*informed* decision making, not data-*determined* or even data-*driven* decision making. This nuance is really important. Data is like wisdom in the Scriptures: it is to be heeded, because we are not gnostics who reject the material world and its wisdom. God has created the material world and pronounced it good. Spiritual life permeates the material world. So we learn from the knowledge we gain in the world while allowing God to flip it on its head when necessary. William Passavant started a hospital against common wisdom, but he drew deeply from wisdom in his model and strategy of healing. He prayed for healing while administering the latest treatment strategies. When common wisdom interfered with God's revelation—like the time Passavant was given an ultimatum with the cholera patients—he obeyed God's voice. Both the best knowledge of the day and the divine inspiration of the Holy Spirit were absolutely essential for his work. Data and measurements may seem out of place in God's redemptive work in the world—but that's only the case when wisdom is allowed to supersede revelation.

We tend to measure what we care about. What we measure, we tend to improve. With an eye toward greater efficiency, most new business owners pay close attention to what goes in and what comes out. Too much is on the line not to. When participation points are sufficient, waste doesn't matter as much to us. But when a vision for real change has gripped our hearts and engaged our calendars and checkbooks, measurements become indispensable, because waste is a major threat. Measuring change is a logical response to fully engaging in a vision to see new life flourish.

Let's say that our congregation decides: "We believe that every child in our community should be able to obtain their God-given potential." So how do we make that happen? First, we define a geography and get to know it inside and out by conducting interviews, inviting people into our homes, and mapping our neighborhood. Our research highlights the need for early intervention with an emphasis on educational and social support for children. That research is supported by a local needs assessment. After much prayer and fasting, we decide that the best strategy is to start a preschool in our low-income neighborhood. Then, with a clear view of best practices and in close collaboration with the families we're working with, we can identify the specific measurements we want to track.

Measurements can lead us to:

- Raise our expectations for real change
- Keep the end in mind
- Help us resist indiscriminate allocation of resources
- Think of programs as a means to an end rather than an end in themselves
- Adapt those programs when necessary
- Enlist people and processes that can help structure our feedback loops
- Increase our impact

Once we're comfortable with the place of data in our work, the good news is that, in the four-part DOOR framework for collective empowerment, the work of good measurements and adapting models is the easiest part. It also happens to be the easiest to overlook and the most likely to derail long-term momentum. The GPS voice recalculating our route after we've veered off path is really helpful on long, circuitous, and unfamiliar journeys that are prone to road closures. When I'm in standstill traffic, I love to hear, "Another route will save you thirty-three minutes. Do you want to take it?" Measuring our work, and making adaptations along the way, is necessary to the overall picture of collective empowerment.

One difference that often separates successful and unsuccessful entrepreneurs is this ability to adjust course soon after launching. Foresight is never twenty-twenty, and once we're in, we need feedback loops and the ability to respond to them.

In general, measurements can be broken down into three types:

- Input: the resources we're investing
- Outcome: the direct results of those investments
- Impact: the indirect results of those investments

For example, if we started a preschool in a low-income neighborhood, our *input* measurements would include our investments of time and money. *Outcome* measurements might include parental involvement in the child's education, higher test scores, and growth in social and emotional skills. Our *impact* measurements might include community-level indicators like child poverty rates, high school graduation rates, college entrance and graduation rates, and juvenile delinquency. We would expect to see those numbers change over time as a result of our work. When asked to define success for the Harlem Children's Zone, a nonprofit in New York City, founder and CEO Geoffrey Canada replied, "The only benchmark of success is college graduation. That's the only one: How many kids you got in college, how many kids you got out."[1] It's a crystal clear outcome measurement that set the stage for potential interim indicators like reading levels and graduation rates.

Since we can't measure everything, the act of establishing measurements is a helpful exercise to clarify why we're doing what we're doing. To everything we do (input), we can ask, "To what end?" What does success look like? For the Harlem Children's Zone, success looks like a college graduate.

As we develop our strategy, a clear view of the end will help shape these measurements. Measurements will flow directly from our strategy. Just keep asking "Why?" and "To what end?" and "Why are doing this?" and "What does success look like?"

Once we have set our measurements, our next step is to determine how we'll actually obtain the data, and what we'll do with it. National foundations engaged in community development work provide helpful guides for both discerning appropriate assessment tools and understanding how best to use them. Two primary classifications for the types of assessments we can use are quantitative and qualitative. A *quantitative* approach is broader in scope and numeric in form, such as descriptive statistics, multidimensional indices (for example, poverty and crime rates), mapping methods, and larger surveys. The benefits of data in a numeric form include the ability to run all sorts of statistical analysis. For example, if college graduation was your primary outcome measurement and you want to understand what strategies best correlate with it, you can run statistical analysis with the various input measurements and interim indicators you track. Just as data is becoming more accessible, software programs to run statistical analysis are becoming more user-friendly.

Qualitative approaches, meanwhile, are more localized and comprehensive, such as focus groups and open-ended questions. They afford space for anecdotes, stories, and opinions that can provide a treasure trove of important data. After-school tutoring participation rates may reveal a promising correlation with college graduation rates, but a family interview can reveal why some children entered a program and succeeded in it while others didn't. This can help us identify potential barriers and unintended consequences of the program.

In sum, measurements are a major part of our feedback loop. As my college baseball coach would often say (just before an unfiltered criticism), "Feedback is the breakfast of champions." We want to make feedback a regular habit of our work. We test our assumptions and think of programs as strategies to accomplish the vision and bring about real change. We don't operate in a vacuum; we constantly learn, evaluate, and adapt our strategies with utmost diligence. We're in the business of life—bringing fullness of life to our communities.

Radiate the vision and empower others
So far, we've looked at the first three of four practices that open the door to collective empowerment. When we define a geography and know it, observe what works and implement it, and operate with measurements and adapt where necessary, we create optimal conditions for life to thrive in our communities.

There are two final and related acts that often become decisive for breakthrough: *radiating the vision* and *empowering others*. In the stories we've looked at so far, you may have noticed that a person's biography is closely connected to the story of that person's work. Hopefully, you've also seen that empowerment necessitates ownership. The act of empowering others best happens in the beginning stages of our work. When we set a vision and determine a strategy in isolation from the community members we're hoping to help, and then try to extend ownership in the implementation stage, we've waited too long. The implication of such involvement at a later stage is "You are part of the problem (even if not directly responsible for it) and I have a solution to fix it that you're unaware of, but I need your help to do it." We may have a sense of best practices and what's needed, but we must not allow such knowledge to supersede the need for community ownership in the early work of praying, researching, vision casting, and strategizing.

For example, if you think your community needs an after-school tutoring program, rather than organize a team to help you make it happen, recruit students who would be potential participants in the program to conduct research on what's needed most. Give them a voice in the process. If you were the student, think about the difference it would make if you were a part of the research process and your voice helped shape the vision and strategy. Ownership of the process provides a huge boost to its likelihood of success.

Here's the catch: That means it can't be about me. My desire for recognition must not get in the way of the need for collective ownership. The work of collective empowerment is best conducted without superstars looking to make their mark on the world. The rise of social entrepreneurship provides ample opportunities to reflect carefully on where and how business and entrepreneurial principles can best be applied to the work of collective empowerment. For example, think about Mark Zuckerberg's oft-repeated phrase, "Move fast and break things."[2] It reminds us to avoid the snares of paralysis by analysis, to expect to remain in perpetual beta mode, to embrace risk, and to act boldly. But people aren't things, and compassion refuses to relate to people primarily as the object of ambition. It's great advice for software development, but not for community development. In the work of collective empowerment, instead of moving fast and breaking things, we need to move compassionately and restore things.

Personal question: Who are you?

The question of this chapter—"To what end?"—can transcend vision statements and measurements of empowerment. It can be a deeply personal question that orients us to an eternal perspective.

Doing the work of smart compassion requires us to consider our own particular faith journeys, and the ways that God is calling us to walk with him.

At the center of our faith is the cross and resurrection. Jesus' death and resurrection divided human history by breaking the power of sin and death over humanity. On the cross, Jesus absorbed our sin and brokenness and opened the door for reconciliation with God and eternal life with him. The cross is also the central symbol reminding us of the relationship between death and life. We too must continually surrender our lives in order to experience the fullness of life God offers us. God's invitation is not merely to acknowledge his existence or do certain things in honor of God or to secure his blessing. The cross is our first destination and the continual centering point for our faith journey with God. Our desires, future plans, resources, self-image, past failures: all of it must be released continually to the Lord with the same expression of faith as Jesus in the garden of Gethsemane: "Not my will, but yours be done" (Luke 22:42). We must pray, "God, you have my permission to rearrange anything necessary to accomplish your purposes." This faith-filled invitation to the Lord to excavate our souls and realign our commitments is the posture that allows God "to do immeasurably more than all we ask or imagine, according to his power that is at work within us" (Ephesians 3:20).

The cross draws us to the core questions of life stewardship: Do I hear God's voice and will I obey it? Are my yeses and nos aligned with God's yeses and nos?

Consider the faith journey of Jacob, who eventually becomes Israel. In Genesis 31:3, the Lord says to Jacob, "Go back to the land of your fathers and to your relatives, and I will be with you." Here's the backstory of this moment: you have a man with little faith, no backbone, and questionable character who's living up to his name, "Supplanter, Trickster." After Jacob steals his brother Esau's blessing and birthright, he runs for his life. Landing at his uncle Laban's house, Jacob gets a little dose of his own medicine. For the next twenty years, he's largely off the grid. During this time, he gets married . . . somehow to the wrong sister! Crazy story; evidently he was so drunk he couldn't distinguish them. Who knows? The historian Josephus tells us that Jacob was deluded by "wine and the dark." It's an absolutely brutal season for the guy. Twenty years of spinning his wheels.

Imagine being the son of a prominent business leader who has promised to hand you the entire empire. But instead of getting your MBA and working your way through the ranks, you start a family squabble that sends you to a farm in the middle of nowhere for twenty years, where you get mistreated.

It would be tempting to assume that Jacob was too far gone for the God-given visions and dreams of his youth to ever unfold. In time, we see that he's not just spinning his wheels. He's learning patience, fortitude, and growing in faith that he'll need in a season to come. In fact, these twenty years become the bridge connecting his old life to the new life that God was calling forward.

The story is seriously comical. Jacob goes from being a homeless seventy-five-year-old with no wife and no kids—classic late bloomer—to a wealthy centenarian with two wives, who happen to be sisters, and twelve kids with four women. That's some serious blended family dynamics. Imagine being their family counselor: "Okay, let me make sure I understand. Your uncle is your father-in-law, his two daughters are both your wives, one of them against your will, and several of your kids have one of two other mothers?"

If you read this story to the end, you realize *he* is the guy picked out to become the father of the tribes of Israel. He's Israel? Don't ever think there's a good reason for ever counting yourself out!

Once Jacob gets the wake-up call to return home, the stages he goes through are instructive. At first, he's compliant, but the trickster is still alive and well. He sends messengers ahead of him to meet his brother first. He's thinking, "Let's send in the fruit trays first, with a little card. Then we'll drive in one of those food trucks with Korean beef tacos he loves. He's always been a sucker for good food. Then, Johnny, you go and tell him that if he doesn't kill me, I'll buy him a sports car and a place on the coast."

The messengers return and say, "We went to your brother Esau, and now he is coming to meet you, and four hundred men are with him" (Genesis 32:6). The Bible says that this makes Jacob greatly afraid and distressed. Probably an understatement. Jacob separates people and animals into groups, thinking, "If Esau comes and attacks one group, the group that is left may escape" (Genesis 32:8). And then he prays. He has spent all day scheming, strategizing, and maneuvering. But before lying down, exhausted, he decides to pray. God has clearly said, "Go and I will be with you."

What God does next is fantastic. Genesis 32:22-24 reads, "That night Jacob got up and took his two wives, his two female servants and his eleven sons and crossed the ford of the Jabbok. After he had sent them across the stream, he sent over all his possessions. So Jacob was left alone, and a man wrestled with him till daybreak."

This is a hundred-year-old man's worst nightmare. He has run from everything his entire life, but here and now, an angel from the Lord won't let him go. I wrestle with my kids sometimes, and I always do it at their level. I give them just enough resistance to make it a struggle. But the angel's goal here is to wear him slap out: "You steal, you run, you cheat, you lie, you manipulate, you have a lifetime's worth of pent-up hostility and misplaced judgment, and I need you to become the man you're called to be and I won't relent until you do. It's you and me now. You're separated from all your stuff, all your people, and you don't have control. It's dark, and I have you right where I want you."

Finally, the angel touches Jacob's hip, and he drops, never to walk the same again. It's as if the angel is saying, "I could have killed you without exerting an ounce of energy." This struggle has one purpose: for Jacob to finally accept his God-given identity and prevail in the right things. During the struggle, Jacob recognizes God's presence and says, "I won't let you go unless you bless me." He finally understands the source of blessing, and the stage for breakthrough is set.

The man asks him, "What is your name?" It's a loaded question with a lot of history.

This time he answers, "Jacob."

The man says to him, "Your name will no longer be Jacob, but Israel, because you have struggled with God and with humans and have overcome" (Genesis 32:28).

It's God's desire to get us to this very place where we come to the end of ourselves. It's always a fight. Our name, the titles that define us, our track record, our desires and dreams for the future: all of it comes to the surface with this question, "Who are you?" In the story of Jacob and Esau, we find three key steps to freedom and breakthrough: receiving forgiveness, extending forgiveness, and accepting your God-given identity.

Faith journeys in the Old Testament often pass through a threshold, like a river or cave, where one's sense of identity changes. For Jacob, the Jabbok served as the turning point. For Elijah and David, the turning point was a cave. In the Old Testament, the cave is often a place of last resort: a gathering place for the disillusioned. When life derails and you're unsure what to trust, where to go, and what really matters, and core theological and identity questions are frightfully blurry, you are entering a cave ordeal. Such places are also where God does some of his best work. Cave experiences can give birth to all sorts of new life.

The cave ordeal: A school for faith development

Every major faith journey goes through a cave ordeal, where we meet our true selves. A cave is that place of proverbial dismantling where new life is forged. But when you're in it, new life isn't what you see at first. You just see what you've lost and what never materialized.

As you get deeper into the work of smart compassion, the scenery starts to look different. When you stop "doing outreach" and start making change, there's a critical juncture you meet pretty quickly. You realize you don't know what you thought you knew. Your ideas and help aren't as groundbreaking or applauded as you secretly anticipated. The work is harder and more complicated than you expected, and it might not even be enough. There's a cruel and painful deconstruction phase that awaits the wide-eyed traveler. Welcome to the cave ordeal!

By becoming a good student of faith journeys, we learn to expect cave ordeals and recognize them as places of both dismantling and rebirth. We learn to see them as transitions rather than destinations and to allow the Lord to excavate our souls, focus our eyes on him, and attend carefully to his voice. A good litmus test for how well we navigate a cave ordeal is how it changes our vision—specifically, what emerges as big and little in our eyes. When our view of God is diminished and people and circumstances loom large, fears and lesser dreams will take hold. Author and pastor John Ortberg describes these lesser dreams as "shadow missions," which aren't full-scale rebellions but rather a partial veering away from commitments. When we recognize God's sovereignty and fix our eyes on him, the same people and circumstances diminish in size and the fears and lesser dreams fail to hook us.

In William Bridges's work on transitions, he describes a predictable four-part process that we undergo when encountering change.[3] The steps—(1) denial; (2) resistance; (3) exploration; and (4) commitment—appear as a U shape. The cave resides at the base of resistance, and our options there are to circle back to denial or press forward into new exploration. Will the necessary death run its course so the resurrected self can arise? Will the illusions and lesser dreams dismantle and make room for God's vision? Will a disembedding from the status quo happen?

Our point of reference during the cave ordeal is predictive for such questions. What and whom do we turn to? What beliefs do we internalize and allow to shape our decisions? The challenge is that caves, by their nature, obscure vision. You seldom get to the cave without earthquakes rattling deep beliefs.

There's an intriguing wordplay in the opening of Paul's second letter to the church in Corinth. In English, it reads like this: "Praise be to the God and Father of our Lord Jesus Christ . . . who comforts us in all our troubles, so that we can comfort those in any trouble with the comfort we ourselves receive from God" (2 Corinthians 1:3-4). In the original Greek, the word *paraclete* (translated here "comfort") is used six times, and the word *thlipsis* (translated here "trouble") is used twice in these two short verses. A *paraclete* was the advocate who walked alongside you with a comforting presence. The Holy Spirit is referred to as our "Paraclete" in John 14:26: "But the Advocate [*Paraclete*], the Holy Spirit, whom the Father will send in my name, will teach you all things and will remind you of everything I have said to you."

Thlipsis, defined as "pressure," "trouble," or "anguish," carried three images in the first-century Roman world. It described these three things: the anguish of childbirth; the act of squeezing olives in a press to extract the oil; and a torture technique in which a large boulder was place on a person's chest until the person suffocated. In John 16:33, Jesus says, "I have told you these things, so that in me you may have peace. In this world you will have trouble [*thlipsis*]. But take heart! I have overcome the world."

Follow Paul's line of reasoning here in 2 Corinthians 1:3-4: Paul begins with the recognition of God's presence in our troubles. God, in all his sovereignty and goodness, walks with us through our "pressing," *so that* we can walk with others through theirs—all in the very presence and power of the living God. What a life-changing perspective on suffering! A study of these two words in the New Testament can completely reorient our perspective on suffering and the gifts we have to offer others.

As we experience God's grace and redemption during *thlipsis* (Romans 5:1-5), we become purveyors of grace and redemption for others. For starters, when you squeeze something, what comes out is what is inside. Martin Luther once wrote, "Whatever (virtues) tribulation finds us in, it develops more fully. If anyone is carnal, weak, blind, wicked, irascible, haughty, and so forth, tribulation will make him more carnal, weak, blind, wicked, and irritable. On the other hand, if one is spiritual, strong, wise, pious, gentle, and humble, he will become more spiritual, powerful, wise, pious, gentle, and humble."[4]

In the cave, we meet our true selves and learn what we believe. As we give space to the Lord for the "dying and rising" work necessary, and press into his grace to suffer well, even when we're forever left with a limp or signature wound, we can become conduits of healing for others.

Angels at the door

At the beginning of the book, I shared a vision of a young family dragging an upright piano into the street after a lethal gunfight. It was inspired by the true story of a family who did something similar. This family had moved into a crime-ridden downtown neighborhood in obedience to a God-given vision. They had renovated dilapidated houses and apartments and provided affordable rent to families, started a house church and weekly Bible studies and prayer meetings, and even launched an award-winning business to employ refugees.

One night, after a steady stream of setbacks, their windows were pierced with bullets. It was a breaking point for them. But instead of self-pity or resignation, they went to the piano and began to sing worship songs with all their windows opened.

A man suddenly knocked on their door and introduced himself and his adopted son. He then proceeded to pray for them and prophesy over their neighborhood. He prophesied that new life would rise up and that they would be a part of it.

To this day, the family views those two men as angels. They never saw them before or since, and the timing and message couldn't have been more God-ordained. Angels or not, those men were well-timed gifts from God!

It's been sixteen years since the family moved into the neighborhood, and their stories are now legendary. Their neighborhood looks nothing like it did when they first moved in. The before and after pictures are adrenaline shots of faith. Their kingdom journals, where they list small and big Jesus-sightings, are reminders of God's presence and ongoing work of redemption all around us. This family's healing presence, radical hospitality, and collective empowerment have now spread far and wide.

When we hear stories like this one, it's tempting to see the outcomes and miss the breakthroughs that led to them. There's always a cave between what is and what is to come, and it's certain that this family went through their own cave ordeals. But it's equally true that God does some of his best work in caves, and an unencumbered yes to God's yes will lead to stories that only God could write.

What is that story in your community?

Gather some people to pray and fast. Drag the piano into the street and worship.

Draw a circle and cry out to God, "Your kingdom here as it is in heaven!"

Open your front door.

Start waging peace.

Acknowledgments

The idea of this book began with a conversation in a prison cell when I was nineteen years old. I had started a weekly service in the state prison near my college in Nashville, Tennessee. Just before a young man was set to be released, we met to discuss his future. I gave him brochures for colleges and phone numbers for agencies assisting with housing and employment. My enthusiasm was off-putting to him, however, and after my pep talk, he slid the papers off the table and said, "You don't have any idea what you're talking about."

He was right, and I'm grateful for that conversation. Years later, Bob Davis, a mentor and friend, always asked a helpful question, "To what end?" I'm grateful for mentors like Dr. Tim Green, Bo Cassell, Dennis Gingerich, Per Nilsen, Greg Kappas, Sam McMillan, Paul and Wendy Vernon, and Keith Weaver. My writing on Barnabas in this book is dedicated to them.

John Troyer and Heather Johns have been encouraging and faithful friends throughout this process. Along with Steve and Ann Weaver, Nita Landis, and Robin Bright, they read early drafts and provided insightful feedback. Robin Bright inspires all who meet her, and I'm grateful she is willing to share her story in this book. I'd also like to thank Brad Fink, Jim and Lisa Halloway, Matt and

Renee Everett, Sue Hook, Chad Woolf, Shannon Litton, and Mark Sweeney.

For more than ten years, our Cape Christian family gave us the most incredible gift and showed us firsthand the beauty of the local church living out Ephesians 4. Mentors at Leadership Network, including Reggie McNeal, Linda Stanley, and Larry Osborne, have been a great gift over the last several years, in so many big and small ways.

I'd like to thank Valerie Weaver-Zercher for her diligence with editing the book. It was quite a feeling to receive drafts back from her and think, "It's what I wanted to communicate and it sounds better." Thanks, too, to Amy Gingerich and the team at Herald Press.

Last, I'd like to acknowledge my brother Brett for being a friend and partner in ministry, and my parents, for doing everything in their power to see redemption in our family tree. My wife, Bonnie, and our three kids—Alex, Elly, and Max—sacrificed much for this book. Bonnie is love through and through.

Notes

2: Compassion + Wisdom

1. Harper Lee, *To Kill a Mockingbird* (New York: Hachette Book Group, 1960), 85.
2. "Blueprints Programs," University of Colorado Boulder, Center for the Study and Prevention of Violence, accessed September 1, 2016, http://www.blueprintsprograms.com/.

3: The Background Moves to the Foreground

1. The tour was sponsored by the organization Time to Revive. More information can be found at its website, www.timetorevive.com. The four movements of healing presence—love, listen, discern, respond—emerge from Time to Revive and other movements.
2. A book that describes life lessons from improv comedy is Patricia Ryan Madson's *Improv Wisdom: Don't Prepare, Just Show Up* (New York: Bell Tower, 2005).
3. C. S. Lewis, *The Screwtape Letters* (New York: Harper-Collins, 2001), 34–35.

7: Babbitt's Table

1. Commission on Children at Risk, *Hardwired to Connect: The New Scientific Case for Authoritative Communities* (Institute for American Values, 2003).
2. Ibid.

8: Boundaries and Your Capacity for Chaos

1. *The Catholic Encyclopedia*, s.v. "Hospitals," accessed September 19, 2016, http://www.newadvent.org/cathen/07480a.htm.
2. Howard Taylor and Geraldine Taylor, *Hudson Taylor's Spiritual Secret* (Chicago: Moody Publishers, 2009), 19–20.
3. Ibid.
4. David Olson, "Circumplex Model of Marital and Family Systems," accessed September 4, 2016, http://www.uwagec.org/eruralfamilies/ERFLibrary/Readings/CircumplexModelOfMaritalAndFamilySystems.pdf.

9: Hospitality from an Eternal Perspective

1. Back cover text from Richard Swenson, *Margin: Restoring Emotional, Physical, Financial, and Time Reserves to Overloaded Lives* (Colorado Springs: Nav Press, 2004).

10: A City of Refuge

1. Seth Siegel, *Let There Be Water: Israel's Solution for a Water-Starved World* (New York: St. Martin's Press, 2015).
2. Paulo Freire, *Pedagogy of the Oppressed*, 30th anniv. ed. (New York: Bloomsbury, 2014).

11: Draw the Circle

1. Jane Waldfogel, *What Children Need* (Cambridge, MA: Harvard University Press, 2010). See also Bruce Bradbury, Miles Corak, Jane Waldfogel, and Elizabeth Washbrook,

> *Too Many Children Left Behind* (New York: Russell Sage
> Foundation, 2015).

2. Gary Slutkin, "Cure Violence." Last modified
   September 4, 2016. http://cureviolence.org/.

12: To What End?

1. Quoted in Helen Zelon, "'There Is No Science':
   Geoffrey Canada's Philosophy" *City Limits*,
   February 9, 2010, http://citylimits.org/2010/02/09/
   there-is-no-science-geoffrey-canadas-philosophy/.

2. Interestingly, in 2014, Zuckerberg announced that Facebook's internal motto had changed to "Move fast with
   stable infrastructure." Steven Levy, "Mark Zuckerberg on
   Facebook's Future, From Virtual Reality to Anonymity,"
   Wired, April 30, 2014, https://www.wired.com/2014/04/
   zuckerberg-f8-interview/.

3. William Bridges, *Transitions: Making Sense of Life's
   Changes* (Cambridge, MA: Da Capo Press, 2004).

4. Martin Luther, *Commentary on Romans*, trans. J. Theo-
   dore Muller (Grand Rapids, MI: Kregel, 1976), 90–91.

The Author

Wesley Furlong is the founder and director of City of Refuge (refuge.life), a network for community transformation, and the director of church development for EVANA, an evangelical Anabaptist network of churches across North America. Furlong holds a master's degree in theology from Emory University and is working toward a doctorate in social work. He and his wife, Bonnie, have three kids and an ever-changing number of foster children. Connect with him at WesleyFurlong.com.

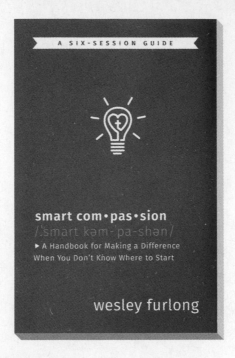